Frauke Kraas | Regine Spohner
Jörg Stadelbauer

111 Places in Myanmar That You Shouldn't Miss

111

T0346470

emons:

Dedicated to our families

© Emons Verlag GmbH
All rights reserved
Photographs by Frauke Kraas, Regine Spohner,
Jörg Stadelbauer
© Covermotiv: shutterstock.com/Xiebiyun
Edited by Alison Lester
English translation: Tom Ashforth
Layout: Eva Kraskes, based on a design
by Lübbeke | Naumann | Thoben
Maps: Regine Spohner
Basic cartographical information from Institute
of Geography – University of Cologne,
Natural Earth (Shaded Relief), ALOS Global
Digital Surface Model (AW3D30,
Shaded Relief) – © JAXA (Japan Aerospace Exploration Agency)
Printing and binding: Grafisches Centrum Cuno, Calbe
Printed in Germany 2019
ISBN 978-3-7408-0714-6
First edition

Did you enjoy it? Do you want more?
Join us in uncovering new places around the world on:
www.111places.com

Foreword

A garage as a restaurant serving tofu specialities, the golden spire of a pagoda next to skyscrapers, grey herons flying up from a labyrinth of reeds, glittering gemstones in a street market, a strenuous ascent to breathtaking views, roads of every possible grade, from unsurfaced mountain tracks for four-wheel drive to well-developed motorways for cross-country buses between the biggest cities – Myanmar, formerly Burma, is a country of diverse contrasts. Fascinating discoveries await, both in the dense crowds of the mega-city Yangon and in the remoteness of the Chin Hills. Culinary delight is to be found in top restaurants and simple street kitchens, and like the Buddhist sanctuaries, the Christian churches and Hindu temples inspire reflection on cultural diversity. One locomotive acts as a memorial to many years of war, another pulls some similarly old carriages over a rickety-looking bridge at dizzying heights. And everywhere you encounter friendly, open people.

A visit becomes a journey back in time: the economy shows extensive irrigated rice production and modern industrial businesses, but also highly specialised micro businesses, working with techniques that are long forgotten or never existed in many other countries in proto-industrial production or in craftwork. Colourful markets as places of pulsating everyday life can be experienced all over the country, while the first shopping malls are being built in the big cities.

Myanmar also offers huge diversity in landscape, from tropical rainforests and palm beaches over broad river landscapes and mangrove deltas to barely accessible mountain regions. There is rich potential for tourism, but its development will require mutual acceptance, adaptation and respect.

111 Places

On the sequence of places described in this book: The order has been consciously chosen in such a way that it can be read like an itinerary through the country. Neighbouring places are thus also side by side in the book. On spelling: There is no unified spelling of toponyms in Myanmar. We use the common international spellings in English phonetics. For many places, rivers and mountains, the names dating back to the British colonial era are also still prevalent (such as Rangun/Rangoon for Yangon). They are sometimes added in brackets for better classification. However, a complete record of the numerous variants of some names cannot be documented.

1 — Singu Min Bell
The lost sound in Shwedagon Pagoda

The deep tones of this now silent bell would have been heard for miles around. In the northwest of the upper platform of Yangon's most important pagoda complex is an open hall under a seven-storey pagoda roof. Here, hanging from a teakwood girder, is the giant Singu Min Bell, also called Maha Gandha Bell ('great sound') due to its size (25 tonnes). Like all the bells on the pagoda terrace its duty was to make the faithful aware, through its sounding, of the commendable acts and pleas of believers. A beater of wood is used by visitors to strike the edge of the other bells and make the masses of bronze sound.

The Singu Min Bell was cast at the behest of King Singu when he visited Shwedagon Pagoda in 1779. The king never saw the bell himself as he had already left by the time his son organised and carried out its casting. When the First Anglo-Burmese War broke out in 1824, the British occupied the Shwedagon Pagoda hill. In 1826 they attempted to remove the bell, pushing it down the hill with the intention of shipping it off on a raft, but the bell – who's lower edge had already been damaged in the tumble down the hillside – slipped and fell into the Yangon River. Worshippers retrieved it and later brought it back to its ancestral place. The parts that had broken off the edge of the bell couldn't be found. To prevent it from suffering any further damage, it is now no longer allowed to be rung. For the people of Myanmar, the bell symbolises the overcoming of the burden associated with British colonial rule.

The Shwedagon Pagoda is an outstanding ensemble of religious sanctuaries in every respect. It stands for the deep anchoring of Buddhism in everyday life, it is a spiritual focus and possesses a highly identifying importance for all of Myanmar. For millions of people, this is the country's religious centre. As such it is also the place that captures the mood of the population with seismographic accuracy.

Address 96°8'55.42" E 16°47'56.31" N, Dagon Township, Yangon | Getting there West
ascent: U Wisara Road; north ascent: Ar Zar Ni Street; east ascent: Bahan Market/Gyar
Tawya Street; south ascent: U Htaung Bo Road; northwest corner of the pagoda plain,
west of Gautama Buddha image, near the Chanthargyi Buddha image | Hours Daily
4am–10pm, last admission 9.45pm | Tip If you visit via the east ascent, you will pass by the
Bahan Market, workshops, the street market and small shops. Look out for snake charmers!

2 Thein Gyi Zay
The 100-year-old market hall

Yangon's most impressive market is to be found right in the centre of the city. The interior of the wood and stone market hall is divided up schematically; Hall A contains around 650 stands, Hall B a good 500. Each stand is made up of a wooden box that covers the floor, is lockable and is filled with fabrics, clothing and other goods. During the day the wooden crate is turned downwards or to the side, the rolls of fabric or bundles of traditional longyis are stacked up high on the sides or piled up in the aisle in front of the stand, so that it is only just possible to pass. A second box is mounted above some stands, which also serves as storage. The wooden construction of the hall leaves lots of space above the stands and thus provides for good ventilation.

You will find almost every kind of merchandise here: fabrics and longyis, terry products, heated blankets in bright colours for the winter months, imported manufactured clothing, household chemicals, paints, fishing equipment, baking ingredients, stones, resins and oils. Both traditional medicines as well as those from the pharmaceutical industry are on offer. The sale of meat takes up its own corner. In the neighbouring halls C, D and E there are household goods, while fruit, vegetables and fish are on offer in the open air in the alleys between the halls.

You won't find a comparable market with such a wide range of products, such long tradition and such deep-rooted trader-customer relationships in Yangon or indeed anywhere else. The special thing about Thein Gyi Zay is its age and the striking degree of its preservation: this is probably the oldest standing market hall in Southeast Asia, and its interior furnishings are also largely preserved in their original condition. Imbued with bustling activity, with life itself, it forms a unique element of cultural heritage that has survived through all the historical upheavals.

Address 96°9'15.49" E 16°46'32.58" N, Pabedan Township, Yangon | Getting there Thein Gyi Zay Block A and B between Kon Zay Dan Street and 25th Street in the block between Anawratha and Maha Bandoola Road | Hours Mon–Sat 6am–5.30pm, Sun 6am–1pm, closed on national holidays | Tip In the early morning you should visit Block A and B in combination with the Morning Market in 26th Street. Climb the stairs of Block C to get a view over large parts of downtown, and a meal.

3 Convocation Hall

Where careers are made

Convocation Hall is – optically, not geometrically – the centre of the country's most important university, the University of Yangon. An inscription is engraved in the foundation stone: the university was founded and spaciously laid out in 1920 under the British. The foundation stone of the Convocation Hall was laid in 1922.

The complex aligns itself on the central axis of Atipathi Road, which runs towards the Convocation Hall, built under the supervision of the architect Thomas Oliphant Foster in 1927. In front, in an almost symmetrical layout, are several seminar and institute buildings as well as multi-storey halls of residence for staff, in parts connected with each other by roofed corridors, which are thankfully adopted in the rainy season. A church, Judson Chapel, was built slightly off the central axis in a style combining elements of art nouveau and art deco between 1931 and 1933. There is also a row of houses on the campus that were built for the university's professors and are still used for this purpose today. The building style is tailored to the tropical climatic and weather conditions: the protruding roof protects against heavy rain, the slats of the windows and shutters promote ventilation, the foyer, which is also the visitor's room, is large and airy. As there are no high-rises on the campus, it is easy to get the impression of being in a green oasis in the middle of the city.

While most of the university buildings have been regularly renovated and painted in the last decade, Convocation Hall stands out with its grey colour ('tropical finish'), which is the result of algae and moss growth; the high humidity and high temperatures during the monsoon season actually lead to the rapid growth and spread of the plants. The reason nothing is done to combat this is based on a modern-day myth: interfering in the appearance is considered as damaging to the university and is supposed to bring bad luck.

Address 96°8'10.06" E 16°49'59.61" N, Kamayut Township, Yangon | Getting there
University campus south of Inya Lake, east of Pyay Road, can be reached via the main gate
on University Avenue Road and Adipati Road | Hours All day | Tip Enjoy a long stroll in
the green of the campus, used at all times of day by locals for walks, and on Inya Lake to
the north – best in the early hours of morning!

4_ 19th Street

Out of old Rangoon

Urban architecture captures and preserves historical developments; we read history from houses. Yangon's old town is made up of 50 quadratic blocks of around 860 by 800 feet, which are bound by wide thoroughfares. A road running from north to south splits each block into two halves. In each of these halves there are two narrow alleys, which are counted from west to east and are only named by their number. Traditional everyday life in Yangon has been especially well preserved in these alleys.

19th Street is part of the city's Chinatown. Yangon's architectural development is easy to retrace by means of examples you can find here. The simple wooden houses that usually have only one storey above the ground floor, which is often used as a shop or workshop, have become rare. Slightly more elaborate are the three-storey business and residential buildings that once characterised the cityscape of the old town, whose wooden wall elements are sealed off by high windows with green wooden shutters. The manner of construction was supposed to enable natural ventilation, which is barely possible anymore in the current conditions of excessive development. Small family businesses are still to be found in these older houses, in the form of shops or small restaurants. Globalisation seems very far away. Two- and three-storey stone structures, sometimes with a mezzanine floor, defined architectural design here until the end of the 1950s.

Since the 1990s the streetscape began to change through new builds, which rapidly grew to eight or ten stories; concrete, glass and glazed tiles were introduced as new building materials and then the first mirrored glass. Developers for ever-taller high-rise complexes were increasingly found. Since 2011, the pressure of the international real estate market has grown, so that the image of the streets and alleys continually changes.

Address 96°8'58.03" E 16°46'30.14" N, Latha Township, Yangon | Getting there Downtown West, 19th Street between Anawratha and Strand Road | Tip The Evening Market in Chinatown between Latha and Lanmadaw Street begins around 4pm; later on the street restaurants on 19th Street in the block between Anawratha and Maha Bandoola Road (Latha Township) beckon.

5 Shri Kali Temple

Colourful ornamental figures in the city hubbub

The goddess Kali – wife of Shiva, one of the most powerful gods – has a terrible countenance, and in the hands of her many arms she bears swords and weapons. Her head is dark blue or black as night, her tongue bright red and stuck out. She roars like the sea, like a raging hurricane, she embodies evil, time and death. But Kali (pronounced with two long vowels) is also incredibly strong, she defeats the demons, bestows protection and blessing. She liberates, she embodies the beginning and creation. She is the origin of everything, the divine loving mother, Maha Kali, the great one, one of the 10 Mahavidyas, the goddesses of wisdom. And she can, according to popular belief, fulfil wishes. This temple is dedicated to her.

The exterior of the colourful temple is in itself fascinating: the several floors of the temple tower (*gopuram*) present deities, guards, wild animals and mythical creatures in a very colourful display. The entrance to the temple is on the east side. Under the *gopuram* – the depiction of the mythical Mount Meru, the centre of the universe – is the *cella*, the most sacred of rooms which only the priests have access to. Here, richly adorned with garlands and flowers, stands the effigy of Kali Ma.

The interior of the temple is atmospherically illuminated by windows in the upper area of the tower. Marble floors, richly ornamented doors, wrought-iron adornments and a very lavish, very colourful interior decoration are all signs of generous donations. To pay for a temple or to make donations to it is seen as a commendable act. In this way the magnificence of a temple allows you to draw conclusions about the prosperity of a community. At the end of the 19th century, the number of Tamil labourers, businesspeople and civil servants increased so much that a magnificent temple was built, by them and for them, in 1871. Today, tourists are also allowed to take delight in its colourful diversity.

Address 96°8'58.03" E 16°46'30.14" N, Latha Township, 295 Kon Zay Dan Street, Yangon | Getting there Kon Zay Dan Street, corner of Anawratha Road, directly north of Theingyi Zay, Block A | Hours All day | Tip On the 20th floor of the Sakura Tower on Bogyoke Aung San Road, corner of Sule Pagoda Road, you can enjoy an impressive view of downtown Yangon, the Shwedagon Pagoda as well as the townships to the north. Purchase of food and drinks required (café 10am–6pm, bar 6–10.30pm).

6_Wardan Jetty
Everyday life between water taxis and freighters

Yangon is one of the huge metropolises on the river or between several rivers, even if the waterfront on the Yangon River has escaped focused architectural and urban development thus far. Access to the banks of the river is virtually impossible on Strand Road, because the colonial-era developments (main post office, Strand Hotel, British embassy, port authority, customs office) were built in front of closed harbour areas. However, the large merchant and transport companies don't define life and trade in the west of the old town, but rather berths for smaller boats do. The boats bring goods, most of which are unloaded by day labourers, or they transport people from the residential area across the wide river and into the delta of the Ayeyarwady to work in Yangon's old town and back. In this section of bustling everyday life there are vendors with street kitchens, and close by along Strand Road some sell fruit and vegetables. The colonial-era warehouses have to a large extent disappeared, making way for a wide road – an anticipation of future developments?

The loads that are hauled off the boats and loaded onto trucks or rickshaws are heavy. Trans-shipment is quick and quiet, but requires a lot of manpower. Little coloured sticks make tallying the piece-work easier: with every bag of cement or rice that a labourer carries off the boat, he drops off one of the small sticks. Some porters even carry double loads on land. This makes it possible to keep track of the number of landed and reloaded sacks of goods.

Rows and rows of narrow, long boats, in which there is space for a dozen people, lie on the banks. They create the link between the banks of the several-hundred-yard-wide Yangon River and beyond. From this perspective, the huge ocean-going vessels that sometimes stop at the piers in the eastern area of the port look like they are from another world.

Address 96°9'15.69" E 16°46'37.97" N, Seikkan Township, Yangon | **Getting there** Port area between Wardan and Lanthit Street, south of Strand Road, continuation of the port area eastwards to Sint Oh Dan Street | **Tip** The atmosphere on the jetties and piers is unique in the early morning and evening; a visit at sunset can be combined well with a walk through the night market between Latha Street and Sule Pagoda Road.

7 National Races Village
The multi-ethnic state in an open-air museum

You don't have the time to visit remote parts of the country and to study the traditional building methods and regional crafts there? Then plan half a day in Yangon for a visit to an open-air museum, where you will get to know the diversity of rural architecture, costumes and everyday life. Don't be put off by the official name, as 'race' stands for 'ethnic groups' here; it refers to all of the ethnicities in Myanmar that are admitted a certain cultural independence. This includes the Mon, Kayin, Kayah, Shan, Chin, Kachin and more.

The site, opened in 2002, can be explored on foot or by bike. Apart from insights into the construction methods of traditional farmhouses and their roofs, it also offers encounters with regional costumes, arts and crafts as well as experiences with the leisure habits of the metropolitan population, as this green oasis on the edge of the mushrooming metropolis is popular among locals too. You find out in passing, through imitation alone, that you do not enter a house with outdoor shoes on, that the shoes stay at the bottom of the stairs that lead to the 'living floor', that the space underneath is used for working, for the animals and for children to play in the shade – beyond the fact that it prevents pets and less desired creatures intruding into the living space. Most of the houses and their gardens are alive: spinning, weaving, pottery, wickerwork and woodcarving are presented here as well as furnishings, musical instruments, work tools, herbs, other crop plants and even a couple of pets. It is also possible to buy small snacks to keep you going between meals and to purchase souvenirs, which you can actually watch being made – from traditional headgear to toys.

When you walk around the village you soon notice that the interests of locals and foreigners are not so far apart: Both wish to combine relaxation in a spacious green area with getting to know different construction methods and handicrafts – an interesting mix of learning and fun.

Address Near Thanlyin Bridge, Yadanar Road, Thaketa Township | Getting there From Yangon on Thanlyin Chin Kat Road just after the junction with Shukhintha Mayopat Road, U-turn before Thanlyin bridge; any bus in the direction of Thanlyin (alight before the bridge) | Hours Daily 7am–5.30pm, admission for foreigners: US$3 | Tip Visit the Shwe Pu Zun Cafeteria & Bakery House (25 (F), Min Nandar Road, Thaketa Township, daily from 8am), around 2.8 miles northwest of the open-air museum, for breakfast or afternoon coffee.

8__ Shin Mway Loon Pagoda
Lonely place of an unhappy love

In stark contrast to the Kyaik Khauk Pagoda, which is visible for miles around, the hidden Shin Mway Loon Pagoda in Thanlyin near the Bago River is only known to insiders. Only a name plaque and an archway before the staircase suggest the existence of the roughly 26-feet-tall golden pagoda, located off the main road on a spur of the Bago mountains and hidden by trees and bushes. The lonely and secluded atmosphere appropriately reflects the mythology of this place – the story of a tragic background, combined with an unhappy love.

Born in a cemetery after the sudden death of her pregnant mother and banished due to the belief that no one born in the cemetery should be allowed to live in the city, the beautiful princess Shin Mway Loon was forced to live alone in a palace on the cemetery above the Bago River. Prince Min Nandar, the only son of the king of Dagon, whose kingdom lay north of the Bago River, fell in love with her. Due to the belief of bad fortune of the princess and a prophecy that said the prince would be killed by an aquatic creature, all contact with her was forbidden. However, equipped with a magic cane given to him by the king of the *nats* (spirits), he crossed the river on the back of the powerful crocodile king Nga Moe Yeik, in order to visit his great love. Scheming among the crocodiles in addition to the carelessness of the prince – he forgot his magic cane – led to the death of the prince in the jaws of Nga Moe Yeik. The princess died of a broken heart.

Once you know this story you certainly look at the hidden pagoda in a different way. Small pools of water with turtles swimming in them are a reminder of the water creatures, and there's also a shrine with a figure and a painting of the princess. If you stand to the far north of the site, you can catch a view of the river, in which this romantic and gruesome story came to its tragic conclusion.

Address 96°14'27.46" E 16°46'40.15" N, Aung Thuka Ward, Thanlyin | **Getting there** From Yangon cross the Bago River on Thanlyin Bridge, around 220 yards past the entrance to Star City turn right into Thati Pathan Road. After around 110 yards look for the sign and stairway to the elevated, slightly hidden pagoda. | **Hours** All day | **Tip** The Myoma Market in Thanlyin and a scattering of colonial buildings, such as the ruins of the Portuguese Catholic church, are very near the pagoda.

9_ Old Royal Palace
Excavating the ghost of a kingdom

Massive, gold-painted concrete columns have recently been erected next to the impressive, excavated stumps of old, dark teak posts, in order to demonstrate the dimensions the palace once exhibited. The teak posts were installed in 1553 as King Bayint Naung erected his new palace in Bago. At the height of his power the extent of his kingdom went far beyond Myanmar's current national borders: what is now Indian Manipur was included, as well as distant parts of today's Thailand and western parts of today's Laos (but not Arakan, which is now Rakhine State).

After the palace was destroyed in 1599, its ruins fell into oblivion. The large audience hall, the Lion Throne Hall (Thihathana), was excavated in 1993; 176 well-preserved teak posts were uncovered, including 136 on which bilingual inscriptions in Mon and Burmese were discovered. The regions and names of ministers and governors, which the clans had sent the king for the building of the hall, are engraved on them. It becomes clear that there have been many capitals over the course of history in the region that is now Myanmar, of which only a few have remained major cities to this day.

In the replica of the palace, now laid out as museum, there are numerous information panels with illustrations of other palaces as well as statues of the three great kings Anawratha (1044–1077), Bayint Naung (1551–1581) and Alaungmintaya (1752–1760). The Lion Throne was also recreated. Here you find out more about the former layout of the city of Hanthawaddy (as today's Bago was called during its foundation). As can be seen to this day in reality in Mandalay or Taungoo, the city of Hanthawaddy was laid out like a chessboard, with the palace complex in the centre, surrounded by an outer moat and a defensive wall and divided into regular quarters. Access was possible via 20 city gates. However, Hanthawaddy's layout can hardly be made out anymore in the streets of today's city.

Address 96°29'35.28" E 17°19'49.2" N, Bago | **Getting there** From AH1 (Yangon–Mandalay Highway) into Bago-Khayan-Thongwa Road, near Shwemawdaw Pagoda right into Myin Taw Thar Road to the Golden Palace grounds | **Hours** Daily 9am–5pm, admission US$4, ticket not valid for the archaeological zone | **Tip** Why not combine viewing the palace with a visit to Shwemawdaw Pagoda, the Shwethalyaung Pagoda, with the second-biggest reclining Buddha in the world and the Kyaikpun Pagoda (Four Seated Buddhas).

10 Kyaikpun Pagoda
Four Buddhas with one world view

South of Bago, a little way from the road, four 90-feet-tall Buddha figures sit back to back and look out into the country, each facing towards one point of the compass. Gautama, on whose teachings modern Buddhism is based, looks to the north; the others are his predecessors. Kakusandha looks to the east, Konagamana to the south, Kassapa to the west. Together they form the all-seeing Buddha, who is also known from some stupas in Nepal. The Kyaikpun Pagoda was built in 1476 during King Dhammazedi's reign. Renovations with bright colours really make the faces (white), mouths (red) and eyes (black), as well as fingernails covered with mirrors, stand out.

The four Buddhas give us an insight into Buddhism's cyclical view of the world and history. The cosmos' creation, duration, dissolution and state of being dissolved are seen as world periods (aeons, *kalpas*), which are followed by the next with the recreation of the cosmos. According to Buddhist tradition, Kakusandha is the first Buddha of the current world period (*badhrakalpa*), followed by Konagamana and Kassapa. Gautama follows in turn, who is himself replaced by Maitreya, before the world period ends. Kakusandha is at the same time the 25th of 29 Buddhas known by name, the fifth of the seven Buddhas of antiquity. The omnipresence of the Buddha figures reminds the people to follow his teaching and to work on the perfection of their own situation, to improve their own karma.

Bago became the capital of the Hinthawady dynasty, which grew out of the Mon kingdoms, in 1365 under King Byinnya U, after which it went on to experience its heyday. King Dhammazedi (reigned 1472–1492) expanded the city, and this also meant that numerous places of worship sprang up in and near the settlement. The Kyaikpun Pagoda was constructed in 1476 on open country outside of the royal city.

Address 96°27'32.42" E 17°18'14.69" N, Bago | Getting there From railway bridge around
2 miles south on AH1, right into Kyaikpun Road | Hours All day | Tip A visit to the
Kyaikpun Pagoda can be nicely combined with a train ride from Bago to Yangon. The
railway station grounds in both cities are worth seeing.

11_Moeyin Gyi Wetland
Bird reserve on the motorway

The entrance to Moeyin Gyi (also: Moe Yun Gyi) Wetland Sanctuary is easy to miss, even though a sign points the way. It leads into the vast hollow, which is taken up by the gradually silting Moeyin Gyi reservoir created in 1978. Its northwestern part was declared a reserve in 1986, in accordance with the international Convention on Wetlands (Ramsar Convention), because millions of migratory birds take a break from their long journeys and find nourishment here. The flat lake is a paradise for bird life with its floating islands made up of plants that are barely fixed to the underlying bed. At the entrance to the sanctuary is a small information centre, which provides an introduction to the natural environment of the reserve with maps and exhibits.

You chug towards the amphibian landscape in a small motorboat. There, where larger, contiguous areas are covered with aquatic plants, the skipper turns the motor off, lets the boat drift or punts it through the apparent thicket, which opens up for the boat as quickly as it closes behind it. Individual storks, herons and pelicans are the first larger animals that you see, before swarms of hundreds of birds fly up repeatedly before settling down again. The list of the birds you can spot is long: little grebes, grey and purple herons, sarus cranes, Asian open-bill storks, sheldrakes, purple swamphens, grey pelicans, jacanas, black-winged stilts and great cormorants can all be sighted. Make sure to listen carefully to the various sounds and melodies which the birds use to communicate with one another.

A few minutes later a section of lotus plants is crossed, and you can watch as single drops of water seem to roll over the water-repellent surface of the leaves. A small pagoda appears to swim in the water, and only the trail of smoke from a factory on the north bank of the lake is a reminder that the area around the reservoir is relatively densely populated.

Address 96°34'49.44" E 17°35'25.96" N | Getting there From Bago to Mandalay exit the AH1 in Botesu village to the right around 19 miles after Bago city centre and 1 mile after Pyinbongyi village, then 0.7 miles on an unsurfaced road to the car park, then 550 yards on foot | Tip You can spend the night at the sanctuary in order to watch the bird life through binoculars early in the morning. Jetty, café, restaurant and accommodation in bungalows (two categories) make up the starting point for all activities (Moeyin Gyi Resort, +95/052/70113, +95/09/73071709).

12 _ 115 Miles

The country's meeting place

The large car park on the Yangon–Nay Pyi Taw–Mandalay motorway has two faces: during the day it is more moderately frequented, and it is mainly cars that are parked under the roofs, protecting them from the sun and the rain. It is different at night, when the long-distance buses stop here to treat the drivers and passengers to a short break. The buses, which seem to rule the motorway, gather here in crowded but orderly rows. One bus after the other is unloaded in an instant, and the passengers use the time for a short visit to one of the numerous restaurants, to take on refreshments or maybe a small meal. Some people might even get out to warm up – the air conditioning systems in the buses are usually quite overpowering. The coming and going of the drowsy travellers animates the large area; the restaurants are well staffed and endeavour to provide speedy service, as the breaks last only 30 minutes. As quick as they came, the buses drive off again, southwards towards Yangon or northwards towards Nay Pyi Taw and Mandalay, and often much further into every corner of the country.

The motorway was built between the years 2005 and 2010 in the course of the relocation of the capital from Yangon to Nay Pyi Taw. But the idea of a 'central transport backbone' in the country is older: at the beginning of the 1950s the Pyidawtha development plan already included the construction of such a north–south axis between the leading centres of Yangon and Mandalay. It serves passenger transport, as heavy goods vehicles are not authorised and has to switch to the less-developed motorway located to the east. Use restrictions and tolls create a two-class society in road transport, keeping away slow vehicles, but enabling a quick connection between the most important cities: it takes express buses just eight hours to cover the 390 miles between Yangon and Mandalay, and five hours for the 230 miles between Yangon and Nay Pyi Taw.

Address 96°23'22.86" E 18°30'32.82" N | Getting there 115 miles north of Yangon on the Yangon–Nay Pyi Taw Expressway, near Phyu Town | Tip You can get to all of the country's larger cities conveniently on long-distance buses. But beware: they are air conditioned and therefore cold – warm jacket, scarf and hat are highly recommended.

13 Hluttaw

The heart of the state government

On 6 November, 2005, Myanmar's capital was relocated from Yangon to Nay Pyi Taw. The reasons were varied. Ever more companies were settling in Yangon, which represented competition in the property market, so that it became almost impossible to increase the number of governmental buildings in the city, and road traffic grew so quickly that appointments could not be met punctually, and in addition, a division between state and economy was desired. In the central plains, roughly halfway between Yangon and Mandalay, in order to refute accusations that the government is subject to the dictates of the economy, a large area next to several existing settlements presented itself as a suitable building site; the Tian Shan mountains as well as the significant east–west route are nearby. Lastly, the fact that relocating the capital has 'tradition' in Myanmar cannot be overlooked: a new governmental location has been sought multiple times through history when dynastic change occurred. Bagan, Taungoo, Bago, Pyay, Amarapura, Mandalay and Yangon have all been capitals before Nay Pyi Taw.

The city is laid out in an extraordinarily spacious way to accommodate growth: wide roads connect the ministries, residential areas, hotels and economic zones and recreational areas. The automobile is the envisaged form of transport, but currently – in stark contrast to Yangon – road traffic is manageable. Still, according to census data, the city has grown to 1.2 million inhabitants – although numerous second homes were most likely included in the count. In the meantime the original villages of Pyinmana, Lewe and Tatkone have become large districts.

The Assembly of the Union, the Pyidaungsu Hluttaw, is to be found in the centre of the city. It is made up of the House of Representatives (Pyiuthu Hluttaw), of which three quarters of the 440 members are elected and the other quarter is appointed by the military, and the House of Nationalities (Amyotha Hluttaw).

Address 96°6'18.4" E 19°46'31.92" N, Zeya Theiddhi Ward, Yaza Htarni Road, Nay Pyi Taw | Getting there From Hotel Zone on Yaza Thingaha Road northwards, 1.8 miles after Water Fountain Park take third exit at roundabout into Yaza Htarni Road, another 2.2 miles reach gates of Hluttaw | Hours Can only be viewed from the outside | Tip Explore the residential area in the district of Ottarathiri where the streets are less empty and the city's life is on show.

14_ Uppatasanti Pagoda

Take the path inside

Every city needs a pagoda; an important city accordingly needs a large pagoda. In the course of the construction of the new capital of Myanmar, the Uppatasanti Pagoda was laid out in traditional Mon style on a mountain ridge between the civilian and military areas of Nay Pyi Taw. It thus follows the design of the Shwedagon Pagoda, which supposedly only outdoes the Uppatasanti Pagoda for size by 20 feet. After the foundation stone was ceremonially laid in November 2006, the structure was completed within three years. *Uppatasanti* roughly translates to 'peace' or 'protection against calamity'.

The visitor reaches a broad, open platform covered in black and white tiles from the east via wide steps or a lift. When visibility is good, you have an excellent overview of Nay Pyi Taw's sprawl between the steep flanks of the Tian Shan mountains over the plains of Sittaung almost to the Bago Mountains. In contrast to Shwedagon, the inside of Uppatasanti Pagoda is accessible. You enter the inner space, where worshippers pay homage to the Buddha figures on the massive central supporting column, through one of the four entrances crowned by tiered roofs. The large inner hall exudes a majestic and calm atmosphere. Places of prayer of various sizes are to be found all around the room.

Plaques recollect the Four Noble Truths from the teaching of the Buddha. The first truth focuses on the existence of suffering, to which all beings are subjected. The second teaches that the cause of all suffering is the attachment to impermanent states and things. The ending of suffering, according to the third, can be achieved if you free yourself from all impermanence. The path that humans must take in order to free themselves from suffering is the fourth truth: the Noble Eightfold Path. It can stretch over several lives and rebirths. The so-called middle path, between self-mortification and indulgence, leads to the cessation of the cycle of rebirth, into Nirvana.

Address 96°10'58.77" E 19°46'15.74" N, Nay Pyi Taw | Getting there North of Yaza Htarni Road, near the Yeypyar golf course | Hours All day. Visiting in the morning at the weekend is especially recommended; in the evening the strong lighting attracts insects like giant beetles and locusts. | Tip At the foot of the pagoda you can buy local snacks and souvenirs from street stalls.

15_White Elephant
Symbol of political legitimation

Elephants are grey and very, very rarely white. Five of these special specimens of splendour are to be found at the foot of the biggest pagoda in the new capital Nay Pyi Taw in their own shelter, where they are cared for, cherished and admired. Three more live in the Royal White Elephant Garden in Yangon. Visitors can feed them with sugarcane and bamboo.

White elephants are in fact albino, missing pigments. In reality they are pink, have light skin, white eyelids and toenails. The specimens living in Nay Pyi Taw come from the forests of the western Ayeyarwady Delta and the Rakhine Mountains. Numerous herds of wild elephants still live here, as well as in the wonderful tropical and subtropical forests of Sagaing Region, Kachin and Shan State, parts of which remain untouched. Estimates suggest that there are still 4,000 to 5,000 wild elephants living in the forests.

In Indian mythology, the god Indra rode a mighty white elephant. In the Buddhist monarchies of mainland Southeast Asia, white elephants are seen as holy, they are symbols of royal power and justice. A ruler who owned many white elephants could boast his people lived in peace and prosperity; many still believe to this day that they stand for a happy future. A white elephant adorned the flag of the kingdom of Siam, for example. Illustrations of the animals are to be found on the murals of numerous palaces, monasteries and temples. Rulers in the Konbaung dynasty in central Myanmar were addressed as 'Hsinbyushin' – 'master of white elephants'.

According to ancient tradition, white elephants cannot work in the service of humans. You can't buy or sell them; at best they can be gifted. Those given a white elephant doubtless enjoyed the favour of the king's grace, but had to take care of the gift at great expense. It has thus come to pass since the 16th century that the term 'white elephant' refers to something expensive to receive.

Address 96°11'7.05" E 19°46'15.87" N, Nay Pyi Taw | **Getting there** North of Yaza Htarni Road, on the east side of the Uppatasanti Pagoda | **Hours** All day | **Tip** Nearby there are small stalls where you can buy pieces of sugarcane to feed the elephants.

16__ Gem Museum

Bling for endless astonishment

The gem museum in Nay Pyi Taw is both a place to wonder in awe and to shop. While the actual museum holds an impressive collection of gems and minerals as well as artworks made with them, numerous merchants on the ground floor offer products from small kiosks that you'd more likely categorise as mass-produced goods rather than exquisite one-offs.

Those who wish to engage in the study of the geology and mineralogy of Myanmar should brace themselves for a very complex structure. The western mountain ranges running from north to south are spurs of the Himalayas, while the Shan mountain region is a part of the Earth's crust that was folded in the Palaeozoic and later pushed upwards. This is where the gems that are so coveted today – from diamonds and rubies, emeralds, sapphires, jade, tourmaline to spinel, amethyst and topaz – were formed from circulating molten masses under the influence of high pressure and high temperatures. They are important export products. Mogok and Hpakant are centres for their mining and trade.

Around half of the exhibition space of the museum serves the classification of minerals and other source materials for jewels (for example pearls), where spectacular individual pieces such as the biggest pearl and the biggest ruby in the world are exhibited. The examples of the artistic processing of the materials are also impressive. In large part these are historic pieces that were once manufactured as a present for a ruler or with a religious background. The artworks express the very distinctive aesthetic of Myanmar, as well as the artists' patience and precision. They are the result of an extraordinary amount of creativity, artistry and manual labour! The basic conditions and technologies used in the mining and processing of gems are not currently on display and interrelated social aspects of the organisation of work are missing.

Address 96°6'56.95" E 19°44'38.06" N, Nay Pyi Taw | **Getting there** East of Yaza Thingaha Road, near the roundabout to Taungnyo Road, northwest of Thapyaygone Market | **Hours** Daily 9.30am – 4pm except Mon and national holidays | **Tip** Several restaurants near Thapyaygone Market are located on the elevation and offer a view of the Water Fountain Garden and the National Landmarks Garden.

17__Puppet Theatre
The story of creation

The old man is fully engrossed, all his senses and passion are involved in controlling the puppets with the cross of wood in his left hand while manipulating the strings with his right hand. He moves the lifelike human figures using 11 to 16 strings. This small theatre is one of only a few authentic venues; the more than 500-year-old Myanmar tradition is preserved here in family ownership. With the lower stage, on which the puppets dance, and the gallery, from where the puppeteers control them, and a few rows of seats for the visitors, there is very little space left for the classical orchestra. U Pan Aye and U Shwe Nan Tin, the old puppet masters, greet the guests in person.

Puppet theatre was first mentioned in 1444 in an inscription on the Htupayon Stupa in Sagaing. In the 18th and 19th centuries elements from the Siamese courts were also integrated into classical Burmese puppetry. During the Konbaung dynasty, the puppet theatre advanced to the leading performance art form in the country; a separate theatre ministry was established to regulate the puppeteers. The puppeteers enjoyed high regard, and helped give viewers an understanding of religious content. In fact, the puppet show did not primarily serve as entertainment and often went on deep into the night.

The traditional puppet theatre begins with creation, symbolised by a musical overture, followed by the appearance of the spirit mediums as the first inhabitants of the world. They are followed by supernatural beings, such as the wizard, and animals, beginning with the horse that flies from the heavens to the Earth. Monkeys, birds, tigers and elephants follow, and finally humans. There is a king, ministers and the Brahmans. Neither the monkey king nor the Himalayan scenery can be missing, nor the battle of good against the demons, nor indeed the alchemist, Zaw Gyi, who lives in the forest. A prince and a princess are always main characters.

Address 96°6'24.36" E 21°58'50.75" N, 66th Street, Mandalay | Getting there Between 26th and 27th Street | Hours Ask at the theatre for show times | Tip Right next to the puppet theatre a simple, open garage restaurant, the Shwe Pyi Moe Café, offers good, authentic Mandalay cuisine.

18_ Geological Garden

Teaching that's far from stony broke

You may be asked at the entrance to the university where it is you wish to go, but the more visitors who ask for the Geological Garden, the more common it should become for the staff to lead them to this true gem – the first of its kind in Myanmar. It was created in 2017 in a collaboration between professors and former graduates of the institute on the occasion of the 63rd anniversary of the Geological Department's establishment. In a country with such rich mineral resources, but which also faces the considerable dangers associated with earthquakes, geologists are of particular value.

What is to be expected of a geological garden? Here almost 150 different kinds of stones are exhibited, with a total weight of more than 80 tonnes. A perfectly practical museum: the exhibits don't need to be guarded in glass cabinets and it doesn't even need its own building. In fact, the pieces of rock are placed in logical order in a beautifully designed ambience, where they can be touched and felt. In the entrance area there are stones of volcanic origin: basalts and microgranites, gabbro from Mogok, hornblende, serpentinite and tourmaline – and an impressive columnar basalt from the Twin Taung volcano that is more than 440,000 years old. In the middle area of the garden there are sedimentary stones: 550-million-year-old greywacke from the Myogyi region, limestone, some with large fossils, dolomite, Triassic alabaster, sandstone and pebbles from Myitsone. Metamorphic rocks are exhibited at the end of the garden: jadeite from Hpakant, augen gneiss, biotite, phyllite. And there is also, displayed separately in front of the entrance to the building, a fine collection of petrified wood and valuable minerals.

The idea was to create an outdoor classroom for students, in order to make geology tangible. Quite rightly the founders claim that the garden, populated with material from the most varied regions of the country, is a national jewel: the Union Rock Garden.

Address 96°5'38.85" E 21°57'26.27" N, University of Mandalay, Mandalay | **Getting there** Enter the Campus from the AH1 on University Road, the access road to the main building, then turn left and behind the Mandalay University turn right to the Geological Institute | **Hours** All day | **Tip** Visit the Main Office Building of the university on Geological Garden with the bust of the founder of the university, U Ko Lay, out front.

19 Bronze Casters
The last of their kind

They say this is the last bronze foundry in Myanmar. At first glance it is an unassuming workshop in the open air. The owner processes orders from all around the world: Vietnam, Korea, Germany. First, the core of the bell is made and smoothed after drying. A layer of clay is applied to this, the 'false bell', the negative of the finished bell. A layer of wax follows, shaped like the later product. The bell case of fine clay is laid on top. Subsequently the form is fired – for eight to ten hours, at 600 and 800 degrees Celsius. The wax melts and leaves behind a cavity. After cooling, the bell case is lifted from the form, the false bell is destroyed, the case removed – and then the cavity is cast with highly heated liquid bronze. After a long period of cooling, the case is broken off, the bell removed, sanded and polished, often for weeks on end – and the right note is hoped for.

Mandalay is the centre of craftsmanship in the country, outshining everywhere else. No surprise: the last kings lived here, and this is where the artists who were captured in the course of successful military campaigns were brought, to work for the court from then on. The constellation of craftspeople includes silver- and goldsmiths, weavers, woodcarvers, masons, jewellers and gold-leaf beaters. Local specialities include fine beadwork, the production of puppets and tapestries and garments embroidered with sequins. In some crafts, several masters still work side by side in close proximity, while others are already dying out, leading to the loss of inherited knowledge and skills.

There is no statistical data on production – craftwork is usually not even mentioned in official reporting on the economic strength of a city. Unlike in other states, Myanmar still possesses enormous, lively and intact traditional knowledge on craftwork – alongside its wealth in raw materials, the greatest endogenous potential during the current process of transformation.

Address 96°4'28.06" E 21°56'9.17" N, Mandalay | Getting there 84th Street in Tanpa Ward (Chanmyatharzi Township), around 580 yards south of Kandawgyi Pat Road on the left | Hours Viewing by arrangement upon arrival or with a guide | Tip There are more crafts to be discovered along the road, for example woodcarving and tapestry producers (Myanmar Tapestry).

20 Oxen Taxis
The ruins of giants

The village of Mingun, which can be reach from Mandalay by charter boat in around one and a half hours, not only offers unique sights, but also a special way to explore them. Instead of a strenuous excursion on foot, why not take the oxen taxi: it is a slow and, because there is no suspension, hard alternative, but it is shaded. First stop on the oxen tour is the unfinished Pahtodawgyi Pagoda, a gigantic, 162-foot-tall base of brick, streaked with splits and cracks since the earthquake of 1838. It is worthwhile taking a walk around the almost 54,000-square-foot ruins in order to gain an impression of its huge dimensions. The builder, King Bodawpaya, a great visionary, had planned a more than 500-feet-tall pagoda, which was to be the tallest in the world. Climbing to the unfinished plateau is unfortunately no longer possible since the powerful Shwebo earthquakes in 2012 have weakened its foundations.

A good 270 yards further north, the oxen taxi stops at the second biggest clapper-less bell in the world. A special experience in sound is to be had if you crawl inside the bell tower and hit the free-swinging, 87-tonne bell in the Buddhist tradition using a thick wooden stick.

Another 330 yards to the north is the bright white Hsinbyume Pagoda, built in 1816. It symbolises Mount Meru, the centre of the world in Indian cosmology. Seven tiered terraces represent the spheres of the seas of the world that surround it. Seven steps lead up to the central stupa, the seat of the deity Indra.

On the leisurely way back to the boat landing you should make a stop at the gigantic earthquake-related stone ruins of the Chinthes at the entrance to the Pahtodawgyi Pagoda. They are protective, lion-like creatures, built out of bricks and overworked with moulding grout. A huge marble eyeball at the feet of the lion's body gives us an idea of how big the Chinthes used to be.

Address 96°1'12.01" E 22°2'53.48" N, Mingun | Getting there By car/motorbike from Sagaing, by boat from Mandalay, oxen taxis await your arrival in Mingun | Hours All day | Tip A visit to the village is worthwhile. Observe life on the Ayeyarwady River and take a look at the 17-foot scale model of the planned pagoda on the riverbank around 330 yards southeast of Pahtodawgyi Pagoda.

21 Sagaing Hill

Meditative view across the water

From the Soon U Ponya Shin Pagoda you can enjoy a breathtaking view over the Ayeyarwady. The neat pagoda with a majestic white Buddha statue, the seemingly endless mirrored halls, the colourful, cool tiles and the clean, painted railings, on which the names of the innumerable donors from all parts of the country can be read in mounted wrought-iron letters, invites you to hang around a while. Families spend the national holidays here, but only a few travellers, mostly day tourists from Mandalay, have discovered it. A good 780 feet above the river, the view moves over the huge expanse of the Ayeyarwady – especially in the rainy season. The river, with its swamped river beds and plains, can then reach up to two miles in width near Sagaing, and up to three miles in width west of Mandalay.

A grandiose river landscape is presented to visitors, with lush green trees, countless white and golden pagodas among them, and huge, heavily laden ships – and the two famous bridges to the south. The old Ava bridge was built in 1934 under the British and rebuilt after the war in 1954. The new Ayeyarwady or also Yadanabon Bridge, with the three large arches, was built from 2002 to 2008. All the road and rail traffic over and beyond the river is concentrated on it.

The regular monsoonal flooding of Ayeyarwady means that the people who settle in the river plains and lowlands have to move temporarily to higher-lying areas. This is why, at the end of the monsoon season, you will see countless huts right next to the large roads, which were built on embankments to protect them from flooding. As such, these simple dwellings are not slums on the periphery of the city, but rather the seasonal relocation to places safe from high water. Some families also bring their animals with them; their zebu oxen graze the embankments bare.

Address 95°59'33.6" E 21°54'6.8" N, Soon U Ponya Shin Pagoda, Sagaing | Getting there Can only be reached by car or by motorbike (around 1.5 hours from Mandalay City Centre), located on the mountain ridge | Hours All day | Tip Take a walk to the many small cloisters on the mountain ridge (beware: there is no signposting).

22___Jade Bead Production

Beads from the shaking board

How do you turn lots of square things round? The answer to this important question is to use a grinder shaking board. The thing is, if you want beads, you have to turn large jade stones into small, spherical pieces. While the cutting of the stone blocks is relatively simple – you only have to carve them into slices, and finally into cubes with cutting wheels – that only gets you so far: small cuboids, perhaps for large wearable beads, but not yet for the more common small beads. These can be rounded with stone tumbling drums, polishing machines, or if necessary – laborious and dangerous for the fingertips – with files and sandpaper. Elsewhere in the country, in Mogok for example, pieces of jade are stuck onto bamboo sticks with wax to grind them. As a result you end up with individual products, not mass-produced goods.

In Sagaing ingenious craftsmen use a special instrument (whether they also invented it can't be determined; they have at least optimised a basic idea): they lay the jade cubes loosely in a metal gridded box that is edged on the outside by an iron ring, and lay this on a rotating grinding wheel. With some pressure from above and horizontal and vertical shaking movements, through which the jade cuboids, which lie only loosely in the box, are continuously joggled into different positions, the cuboids are ground, with the addition of water, evenly round. Then the freshly rounded jade beads only have to be polished before they leave the workshop and reach the international market. Huge amounts of jade cross the borders every year. But the beads are not given the final polish in Sagaing, rather in special workshops in Mandalay, Bangkok or China. Jade is sensitive after all. It is either nephrite, mostly green because of the mineral actinolite but also brown and yellow, or the scarcer jadeite. This is shinier and is made up of several minerals, pyroxenes; they are also mostly green, but also white, blue or pinkish.

Address 95°58'15.04" E 21°52'43.96" N, Sagaing | Getting there From Sagaing station around 1 mile on Market Street to the west | Tip Small shops in the neighbourhood offer jade products at low prices.

23 Twin Ywar Lake

Local recreation in a crater vent

If you know what it is, you'll recognise it straight away: almost perfectly round in shape, with steep vertical edges and a green shimmering lake in the middle – a textbook crater. Twin Ywar crater is in fact just one of a long row of craters that run southwest-northeast a good 20 to 40 miles away from Monywa as the crow flies. The highest, at up to 650 feet, and biggest in the row, the Twin Taung crater, is to the east; the other large craters are west of the Chindwin River. As there are no signs of an eruption during the last 10,000 years, experts speak of dormant volcanism. Strictly speaking, this is a series of explosion craters from the Pliocene and Pleistocene epochs. Four of the craters contain lakes, in which the naturally occurring cyanobacteria spirulina (sometimes also referred to as algae) is cultivated, and after the harvest dried and processed into dietary supplements or medicine. However, human overuse in recent years has had a strong negative impact on the water quality of the lakes, resulting in diminishing spirulina harvests.

For the local population, Twin Ywar Lake represents a wonderful local recreation area, where they meet for picnics or fishing at the weekend. Arable and cattle farming is practised in the craters nearby, which have silted up in the meantime. Groups of people in search of relaxation travel here at the weekend, even from Sagaing or Mandalay, a good four-hour journey away.

A range of manifestations of volcanism, alongside this series of craters, can be observed in Myanmar. Especially well-known are the 4,980-foot-tall Mount Popa and the 2,156-foot-tall volcanic cone Popa Taung Kalat, on whose peak the Tuyin Taung Pagoda is located. The last eruption appears to have taken place around 500 BC. Less well known are various mud volcanoes, for example near Minbu (near Monywa) or Saichon (near Kyaukphyu). They are created by the discharge of methane gas from the interior of the Earth.

Address 95°1'17.75" E 22°16'53.66" N | Getting there From Monywa centre around 5.5 miles on the highway to the northeast, then to the left over the Chindwin bridge; follow the Monywa-Kalewa Highway for 14 miles, then right on unpaved road to Twingon village right on the crater edge (around 3.5 miles) | Tip In the centre of the village there are simple restaurants serving local food.

24 Myinkaba Lacquer Village

A whole lotta lacquer

The young women engrave delicate patterns in bowls and cups with great precision and speed using simple styluses. For generations, the resident families have cultivated specific patterns, style elements and ornamental series. These include views of Buddha, mythological figures and signs of the zodiac as well as demons and guardian spirits, temple buildings, animals, geometric or floral decorations. Various 'artist's schools' developed since the Konbaung period (1752–1885). Bagan is well known for its flat-sanded coloured lacquers, which are created in individual layers of colour, one after the other.

The village of Myinkaba, south of old Bagan, is one the most renowned production locations of lacquerware: a majority of households obtain above-average income, additional to seasonal employment in tourism, through its production. Alongside the manufacturing of primary products – for example the harvesting of bamboo or the creation of raw forms – the lacquer products must be processed through the application of layers of lacquer, colouring, sanding and decorative engraving.

On a walk through the village you can follow all the steps in the production process. The poisonous raw lacquer, extracted from the lacquer tree (*Gluta usitata*), which grows wild in Shan, Chin and Kachin State, is kept viscous through exposure to the sun or heat lamps and strained through fabric sieves several times, while continuously being stirred, thus freeing it from contaminating substances. The body of a vessel is sanded flat and polished. The vessels are subsequently primed with raw lacquer and between 3 and 21 layers of lacquer are applied, each interrupted by several days of drying in cool, humid (for a hardening of the lacquer) and dust-free cellars. This means that the whole production process can stretch over many weeks, or even months.

Address 94°51'30.61" E 21°9'14.83" N, Myinkaba (Bagan, UNESCO World Heritage
Site since 2019) | Getting there North of Manuha Temple, just before creek turn left onto
unpaved road, approx. 220 yards to workshop | Hours All day | Tip While in Myinkaba,
you can also view Manuha Temple, the very old Nan Hpaya Temple, a stone inscription and
the art of sand painters at the Gu Byauk Gyi Pagoda.

25__Mine Lake

Welcome relic of an unsuccessful explosion

It appears as though part of Mogok lies idyllically around a lake. However, the expanse of water is not, in fact, the remainder of a once larger, natural lake, but rather an unintended creation, which is now integrated scenically into the cityscape.

The search for rubies and sapphires is always hindered seasonally by monsoonal rainfalls. In order to divert the undesirable accumulation of water in Byon above the city, drainage channels and tunnels were laid out. The most important drainage tunnel was built at the start of the 20th century by the British engineer A. H. Morgan. This tunnel led through the bedrock, 100 feet under the city, for over half a mile, preventing further flooding and exposing a new extraction site in the valley above the city. However, in 1925 the summer monsoon rainfall was especially heavy, which led to flooding, and serious damage was done to the drainage tunnel. It was therefore decided that year that Morgan's tunnel should be detonated. That's one explanation for the urban body of water. According to another, the British blew the tunnel up so that the mine couldn't fall into unfriendly hands. The consequence was that the site unintentionally subsided and quickly filled up with water. Today's lake, a distinctive feature of the cityscape, is the west part of the flooding area that was created.

As there is now little underground drainage, there are considerable fluctuations in water levels in the city. The Yeni River, which flows through the eastern parts of the city, as well as the Yebu flowing from the northwest, are constrained by concreted beds, while the water level of the mine lake fluctuates with the weather and discharge conditions. The northwest and northeast sides of the lake are lined by popular restaurants, and the main road runs along the south and east side. Waterfront reinforcements and a kind of promenade are intended to make the area by the lake into an attractive recreational space.

Address 96°30'6.19" E 22°55'4.47" N, Mogok | **Getting there** South of the Mandalay-Myitkyina Highway, west of Mogok-Kyaukme Road (NH31), near the Mogok Hotel | **Tip** A good overview of the lake and large parts of the city can be had if you climb the hill south of Mogok Hotel to Padamyar Pagoda. A particularly special atmosphere in early morning.

26_1,000 Buddha Monastery
The heart of the Chinese community

One of the caves of Mogok hosts the Monastery of 1,000 Buddhas – one that is maintained by the Chinese community. Ten nuns live here and take care of the monastery and its visitors. Countless large and small, mostly identical-looking Buddha figures stand on altars and in recesses, and hang up high on the rock. Nearby is a large, multi-storey Chinese language school, financed by Chinese sponsors. More than 1,000 pupils receive Chinese lessons here, in addition to normal school, during off-peak times, at weekends and in the school holidays.

The Chinese community in Mogok and the surrounding area apparently comprises up to 80,000 members – no one knows the precise numbers, but the wealth and influence of the Chinese is unquestionably considerable.

Already in the 13th century – as European explorers reported – Chinese merchants in Mogok sold rubies to Europe. Chinese labourers immigrated in huge numbers at the start of the 20th century, as they were needed in the course of the colonial exploitation of mines. These included Shan Chinese, but also countless Chinese from Yunnan and the provinces of Guangdong, Guangxi Zhuang and Fujian. The immigrants were enticed to travel both through word of mouth and through systematic recruitment. The industrious, loyal labourers, accustomed to hardship, were greatly valued among the British. Many of the Chinese in Myanmar today are descendants of refugees who fled to the country after 1949 to escape Mao's troops. Today retailers and investors from China follow in unknown numbers, buying raw materials, importing goods and securing mining rights. They are increasingly involved, as sole owners or in joint ventures, in mining. These companies operate with expensive, international technology, heavy equipment and specialised professionals. They already shape city life far beyond the monastery grounds.

ဘုရားတစ်ထောင်
လိုက်ဂူ

寶井
千佛洞

Address 96°30′31.85″ E 22°55′38.38″ N, Phaya Tha Thauk Monastery, Mogok | Getting there Past Padamyar Market in Aung Chan Thar Ward to the northeast to the Mahar Muni Pagoda on the mountain, entrance to the rock monastery on the south side near the Chinese school | Hours All day | Tip Right next door is a large Chinese private school. A cluster of colonial houses in Myoma Ward between Chan Thar Gyi Pagoda and Mogok Lake, especially in the quarter west of Martyr's Monument, is worth seeing.

27___Gemstone Paintings
Shaken, not stirred, but glued

Little pots cover the tables, holding colourful stones, ground gem-stone sand, lacquers and glue. At the tables the 'painters' sit, mostly women, bent over paper on which they stick stone after stone using tweezers, or sprinkle ground gemstone sand from rustling paper bags twisted into rolls. With skilful dexterity, their efforts bring forth images, creating motifs of every kind, shape and size over weeks of patient attention.

This area is known for its traditional, highly sophisticated products, including these handmade gemstone paintings, which are bought and sold throughout the country as popular and valuable presents. The raw materials are on one hand small precious and semiprecious stones and on the other filing/sanding waste, separated according to different stone types and colours, which are ground into fine stone grit or powder. Work-intensive coloured pictures are sprinkled, placed and glued using both. The motifs range from representations of Buddha or saints, religious places, portraits of well-known celebrities or post-card motifs to typical landscapes or tourist destinations.

The population of Mogok lives almost exclusively directly or indi-rectly from mining, processing and trading in gems: alongside the operation of opencast and deep mines there are hundreds of craft workshops, most in family ownership, in which gems are cut, sanded, polished and processed into jewellery or pictures. Innumerable busi-nesses offer raw or processed precious and semiprecious stones, jewellery produced in Mogok and processed products or items of equipment. This equipment ranges from pans, shovels and ropes for mining to torches and ultraviolet lights for screening the finds, to cutting gear, magnifying glasses and measuring instruments for the preparation and processing of gems. Some tools were invented in the workshops themselves, which are often family businesses, others bought and used over decades.

Address 96°31'2.03" E 22°55'45.82" N, Mogok | Getting there From Mogok Lake around 1 mile northeast on the Mandalay-Myitkyina Highway; ask here for the gemstone workshops | Tip There are street gem markets (south of Mandalay-Myitkyina Highway, between the Martyr's Monument and the old cinema) and large stationary gem markets (Gems Bazaar with many small stalls and open trade northwest of Mandalay-Myitkyina Highway between Peik Swe and Aung Chanthar monastery on the canal). Beware: only buy gems from licensed merchants.

28__Street Gems

Rubies from a bag

The street is suddenly full of people. A few minutes earlier this was still a completely normal street in a residential area, nothing to suggest that a market was to open here a little later. Vendors and customers meet to address one another, disorderly, apparently randomly. A market of possibilities. You enter into conversation with each other, coming straight out with the question of what you wish to buy or what you have to offer. It quickly becomes clear whether your counterpart is seriously interested, only wants to look, or if they are at all knowledgeable about things to do with gems. Soon someone pulls a plain paper envelope from their jacket pocket and opens up the contents: rubies, emeralds, moonstones – what does the discovery cost?

Open-air gem markets take place daily in several places. Here, finds are traded and swapped. Every day in Kyatpyin there is the 'Aung Thit Lwin' morning market and the 'Pann Ma' afternoon market. The buyers can check the stones for authenticity, inquire into details of the location and circumstances of the find, and illuminate and screen them with magnifying glasses and ultraviolet torches. The negotiation process can become protracted, over several days even, during which other experts also become involved. Truly valuable pieces, however, either raw or polished, are more likely to be found in small shops or at specialised dealers, with whom you establish a connection via a middleman.

The sale of gems to foreigners is only allowed through licensed and authorised merchants, but it is also tolerated on a small scale in the street markets. There is no need to worry about counterfeits: there are so many specialists around who can't be deceived, and so much real material is in circulation, that anyone who brought false goods into play wouldn't have a chance to gain access. Trust is the ultimate currency.

Address 96°31'2.03" E 22°55'45.82" N, Kyatpyin | Getting there Kyatpyin centre, road running east to west north of the pagoda with the 10 golden stupas (west of the NH31) | Hours The market only takes place twice a week, enquire about exact times locally | Tip On the west end of the street is an old café with old newspaper reports on the wall.

29___Mining Village

Neighbourhood in an excavated landscape

The landscape in the surroundings of Mogok has been transformed by hundreds of years of the mining and timber trades. You can see it immediately if you drive past the numerous churned-up opencast mines, in which gem-mining was or still is carried out. You can sense it when you walk through the villages and districts of Mogok. Settlements had to be relocated and re-established several times in the course of expanding mining, especially at the beginning of the 20th century. If houses are similar in size and furnishing, this is usually a sign that a settlement arose at the same time and so has often been relocated.

Open cracks, stud holes and bulldozed slopes on many mountain flanks testify to intensive mining activity. Many hillsides have been cleared and now exhibit sparse secondary and tertiary vegetation. The extraction of timber dates all the way back to the pre-British period: for example, in the middle of the 19th century the local rulers, the Sawbwa, had to send 100 teak trees to King Thibaw in Mandalay every year as a gift to the palace. Soil loss and slope erosion make reforestation difficult. Occasionally you can see agricultural areas, some terraced, on which arable farming is practised; on some slopes you can still find the traditional Taungya culture, a form of slash-and-burn agriculture widespread in Myanmar.

Mining activities have many different consequences. They have led to a lowering of the water table. The provision of drinking water was already a problem in the British colonial era. Streams and rivers often develop an altered course. The water collects in the countless silted-up hollows, burrows and pits during the rainy season, spreading illnesses such as malaria, dengue fever or chikungunya. The people must manage such challenges to both ecology and personal health, for the use of these precious raw materials.

Address 96°24'27.63" E 22°53'51.63" N, Kyatpyin | **Getting there** Kyatpyin, around 6 miles west of Mogok | **Tip** The Pint Ku Taung Pagoda offers itself as a lookout point above Kyatpyin; it can be reached by foot from the south and east, and you can get near the pagoda by car.

30 Slash-and-Burn Islands
Light green in dark green

The road itself is remarkable. Running between Pyin Oo Lwin and Mogok, it was developed a few years ago, mainly following the crest of a mountain range, but – to prevent more expensive bridge construction, which is also vulnerable in the monsoon season – it was laid out on a winding route with numerous short climbs and drops. As the mountain range is not continuously forested, spectacular views of the landscape are to be glimpsed time and again along the road. Only a few settlements near the road indicate that you are not in a completely deserted place.

Where the slopes of a valley retreat a little and a small basin forms in the void, fine material silt and water can be dammed up. Fertile soil ideal for cultivation accumulates here. Even during the dry season there is water available for agriculture in small rivers. Here rice paddies are laid out, their light green contrasting with the darker, forested slopes.

But these slopes are not uniform either. Light areas of around one to three hectares can be made out, on which there are no trees. Others display the re-growth of forests, and others again are covered in forest. These are the hallmarks of tropical forest-field crop rotation, or slash-and-burn cultivation, called Taungya culture in Myanmar. The forest on such an area is first cleared in the dry season, then burned, in order to use the nutrient-rich ash as fertiliser for plants. The fires are controlled so that they don't get out of hand and additionally tall, so-called 'achiever' trees are purposely left standing during the clearance, in order to accelerate the later reforestation of the area. The farmers then sow special strains of rice, millet, soya and maize in the warm ashes shortly before the start of the monsoon. After two to three years of agricultural use, the fields are left to themselves, bushes and trees return, and after a few decades the forests can be slashed and burned once again.

Address 96°32'46.38" E/22°49'5.81" N, Pong Hkaw | **Getting there** Around 10 miles southwest of Mogok on the road from Mogok to Pyin Oo Lwin, not always accessible due to landslides and construction | **Tip** Rice as a basic foodstuff is not only cultivated on flooded fields in valleys, but also as dry rice on mountain slopes.

31 Former Shan Palace

Forgotten?

You really have to ask the way in order to find the place. Then you can only look from the locked gate into the grounds of East Haw, the former Shan palace, built in 1924, hidden behind dry trees in an overgrown park: a stately home in distinctive Edwardian style – apparently abandoned. If you know anything about the history of this Haw and its inhabitants – as far as it is known – you will inevitably ask yourself: how present are these stories and events in the individual and collective memory of the people in Hsipaw and Shan State? As the wife of the last Saophalong, Sao Kya Seng, prince of Shan State's Hsipaw, Austrian-born Inge Eberhard was called 'Mahadevi Sao Thusandi', 'Heavenly Princess'. She has lived in the USA since leaving Burma in the middle of the 1960s; the fate of her husband remains unclear to this day.

The history of the family represents the ups and downs in the relationships between Shan and Burmese, as they are integrated in the sometimes difficult higher-level problems of the relationships between state and regions, the distribution of resources, land, influence and power in a multi-ethnic state and the question of how to deal with such varied interpretations of history.

For East Haw and the other Haws still standing in Shan and Kayin State, the question arises as to how the cultural heritage can be dealt with in a forward-looking, conciliatory form. Many buildings deserve some attention, as they are overgrown by vegetation and tormented by the rigours of numerous monsoon and dry seasons. The financial capabilities to adequately preserve the buildings are missing. The extent to which an awareness in history, culture and traditions has grown among locals, as well as open-minded foreign tourists, has meant historic buildings have taken on increasing importance. A conversion into a museum is conceivable, but it is hard to obtain historic exhibits and documents.

Address 97°18'19.72" E 22°37'35.58" N, Hsipaw | Getting there In Hsipaw from the Mandalay-Lashio Road (NH3) turn left by the restaurant A Kaung Kyite, around 0.7 miles after crossing the Myitnge-Zu River turn right, follow the road to the gate | Hours The building is in private ownership, but viewing seems to be possible recently by arrangement. Inquire yourself locally. | Tip You can take an unforgettable train journey from Hsipaw to Mandalay.

32 Kuan Yin San Monastery
Crowning the slope

All of the many, many monasteries in Myanmar are special, each one in a particular way. The Kuan Yin San monastery with its temple and outbuildings is reportedly the largest of its kind in the country. Built in 1950 and renovated several times, it sits in a prominent position, crowning a slope over the city. The whole monastery complex, taking in a good 325,000 square feet with several large gates, through which you must ascend to reach the temple, impresses through its stunning dominance alone. Larger-than-life temple guard statues pulling dreadful faces with dark green or deep brown skin and powerful canines instil all unwanted visitors with a sense of respect.

More than 40 nuns and monks live here permanently on an 'island on the island', cared for and embedded in the surrounding residential quarter, which is also almost exclusively inhabited by Chinese. According to estimates, Chinese make up around 60 per cent of the city's population, but the proportion is probably higher, as numerous Chinese families, who can't even speak Burmese and have clearly immigrated recently, live in the new neighbourhoods – for example below the monastery or in the suburbs. You can easily determine the ethnic background of inhabitants just by looking at their houses: Chinese characters on doors and gates, red lanterns, stickers of the current Chinese sign of the zodiac or yin and yang symbols to appease evil spirits.

Lashio, situated at an altitude of around 2,800 feet, lives off nationwide trade and is an administrative centre and a university city. Lashio was the starting point of the Burma Road, over which the Allies tried to secure the supply lines from India in support of Chiang Kai-Shek's headquarters in Kunming. The link is once again growing in importance: Lashio's importance as a trading hub has grown massively since the motorway from Mandalay to the Chinese border-crossing town of Muse was developed.

Address 97°45'19.91" E 22°55'34.18" N, Lashio | Getting there On NH3 around 2 miles after Lashio Highway Bus Station turn right into Mandalay Street, after 1.5 miles right onto Dhamma Yeiktha Street, after around 700 yards left onto 10th Street, around 600 yards to the gate of the temple on the right side | Hours All day | Tip The view over the city from old Sasana Pagoda, located on a hill in the central urban area, is very beautiful.

33 Hot Springs
In hot water

If you submerge them for long enough they'll turn as red as lobsters. We're talking about feet. The hot springs of Lashio are exactly as the name suggests. There, where the springs emerge from the ground, the water is boiling hot and cannot be entered. But where it is accessible in the many different watercourses and pools the springs feed – left natural like a gently flowing stream or contained in cooling concrete basins – it can be used in many different ways: for washing clothes, for paddling or bathing and, in separate areas, for extracting drinking water. You will see men and women both standing at the washing troughs washing clothes, because in Myanmar everyone is traditionally responsible for washing their own laundry, and the children usually play around them. Bathing, on the other hand, is of course separated by gender. So, depending on the time of day, you can, for example, come across groups of different ages chatting in the women's pool (dressed in longyis of course). A group of elderly Chinese women meets here after 5pm, as they have apparently done every day for five decades, nowadays to combat rheumatism and arthrosis.

Recently, efforts have been made to additionally upgrade the site with simple restaurants and street kitchens as well as small souvenir shops. There is also a VIP room, just in case. It is precisely the largely undeveloped and slightly unrefined character of this pretty place that makes it so attractive: A small stream has been left as it was, with picturesque meadows on its banks. There is even a small playground that will make any age group happy. But the bathing pleasure is greatest on cold winter mornings, when temperatures sink to between 5 and 15 degrees Celsius and the morning mists give the atmosphere quite a damp unpleasant note: you can hardly imagine a more pleasant place in Lashio – and unlike electricity and the Internet, there are no blackouts in a hot bath.

Address 97°46'27.95" E 22°59'30.5" N, Lashio | Getting there NH3 out of town, past the airport, to Silver Sky Hotel, turn off to the left, entrance to the thermal springs after around 0.8 miles | Hours All day | Tip A visit to the street kitchen on the edge of the site is recommended, especially at sunset.

34__Gokteik Railway Bridge
Riding an iron horse over trestles

It wasn't long after the film *The Bridge on the River Kwai* came out in cinemas in 1957 that the toy-making industry started selling building kits with which children could recreate the spectacular bridge in miniature. You may feel reminded of this construction when you see the train on its way across the Gokteik viaduct.

Bridge-building engineers talk of trestle bridges and they are mostly constructed for railway building. Several identical trestles, originally made of wood, later of profiled steel, are lined up, one after another. The lower sections of the masts might remind you of electricity pylons, but they are constructed so closely to one another that they can be connected with each other at the same height. Then the track just has to be laid over the trestles, and the bridge is finished – without a footpath for workers maintaining the bridge.

The Gokteik bridge, which carried the single-track railway line between Mandalay and Lashio, was built in 1899/1900. It was constructed by the Pennsylvania and Maryland Construction Company, which had acquired the necessary know-how for bridge building in mountainous areas with the installation of railway bridges in the North American Appalachians. The 2,260-foot-long structure was supposed to contribute to securing the expansion of British colonial rule to the east, and therefore initially had primarily strategic importance. It was later recognised that such a bridge construction was at risk in the case of emergency, and an alternative route was even created in the 1970s, but this was soon abandoned. Today the original route over the viaduct is still used, but the trains, pulled by diesel locomotives, drive slowly, because routing in mountainous terrain is extremely complicated and large differences in altitude must be overcome in several loops both north and south of the Man Pan Hse River.

Address 96°51'34.51" E 22°20'35.06" N | Getting there On the railway route from Pwin Oo Lwin to Lashio between Nawnghkio and Gokteik over the Nam Pan Hse Chaung | Tip The journey on the Mandalay-Lashio Road (NH3) through the steep valley of the Nam Pan Hse Chaung is also an experience; the gorge is negotiated via a number of tight switchbacks.

35 All Saints Church

World War commemoration

The Queen's Royal Regiment, the King's Own Scottish Borderers, the 10th Gurkha Rifles, the 2nd Battalion, Royal Scots – they all contributed to the renovation of the Anglican All Saints Church, as is stated on a bronze plaque in memory of the victims of the wars. The plaque commemorates the first church service in March 1945 after three years of Japanese occupation and how the soldiers had the chance to recuperate in a 10-day break from the front in Maymyo after six months 'in the hardest and most inhospitable conditions in the world'. The 2nd Battalion of The Royal Berkshire Regiment keeps the memory of the soldiers who lost their lives between 1899 and 1950 alive. Many British organisations are still involved in charity in Myanmar, individual battalions supporting a range of causes, for example children's aid, Allied war veterans or refugees from Myanmar.

The church, built of bricks in 1912, consecrated in 1914, completed with a steeple in 1927, and now splendidly renovated in bright red, was the hub of the British community in Maymyo. In 1896, after the Third Anglo-Burmese War, the British major general James May of the 5th Bengal Infantry had a garrison town built by the village of Pyin Oo Lwin, a typical hill station at 3,450 feet. The summer residence of the British administration guaranteed cool recuperation from the hot lowlands. Maymyo, the town of May, received a clock tower, schools, hospitals, churches, botanical gardens and a rowing club. Numerous houses in British country house style, horse-drawn carriages as well as the high proportion of Indians and Nepalis still represented here recall this past. The town, which has since been renamed to the original Pyin Oo Lwin, is a recreational destination for the citizens of Mandalay and the seat of several military academies to this day. The growing number of second homes is evidence of the high standard of living.

Address 96°28'16.86" E 22°1'32.95" N, Pyin Oo Lwin | Getting there On the NH3 from Mandalay, past the Defence Services Academy entrance gate with the monument in front, to the roundabout, first turnoff right onto Ziwaka Street, after 220 yards on the left side | Hours All day | Tip It's worth taking a ride through the city in one of the colonial horse-drawn carriages as well as viewing the carriage workshops between Mandalay-Muse Highway and Cherry Road east of the junction of Highway and Circular Road – one of the few places in the world that still produces them.

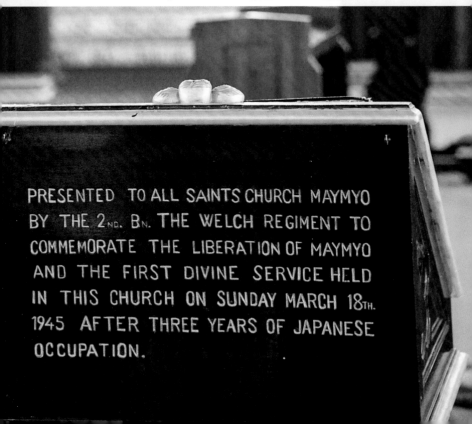

36__Coffee Plantation
Golden Shrimp coffee

It has only begun to spread in the past few years, but with impressive speed: the new coffee and café culture. This in a country which has traditionally drunk tea and in which simple tea shops are to be found on almost every street corner, symbolising encounters and communication. People's consumption of coffee in general and specifically the opening of cafés in the cities are like a yardstick for the advent of the market-oriented economy. It is a transfer of globalisation to the middle-class population. But the coffee innovation not only changes the drinking habits but also the behaviour of the people towards 'the little in-between snack': lately, ever more people – especially in the cities – are prepared to pay more for new kinds of sweet pastries, biscuits and cakes. They have 'modern' designs and are hygienically packed – marble cake and crunchy rolls are conquering the market. Instead of fruit and fermented tea, the present you now bring as a guest is coffee and cake. New ideas are spreading with coffee machines and cake counters.

Pyin Oo Lwin is the country's coffee-growing paradise: missionaries brought the plants with them and began experimenting with its cultivation in the area around Myeik and Dawei, initially in vain. The breakthrough was achieved in 1930 in what was then Maymyo (now Pyin Oo Lwin). But only since the end of the 1990s has production grown significantly. The mellower Arabica varieties outweigh the strong Robusta beans; blends are growing in the customers' esteem. Now new regions, which previously only produced for local demand, are joining in, for example Tiddim in Chin or Thandaung Gyi in Kayin State. A traditional family-run company stands out among the many vendors in Pyin Oo Lwin: Shwe Pa Zun ('The Golden Shrimp') not only supplies coffee beans, but embellishes its range with dairy products, pastries, desserts, jams – and macadamia nuts. A new star in the sky of quality consumables?

Address 96°26'55.15" E 21°59'31.06" N, Pyin Oo Lwin | **Getting there** On the NH3 from Mandalay, past the Defence Services Academy entrance gate with the monument in front, to the roundabout, first turnoff right onto Ziwaka Street, turn right after 760 yards, after around 870 yards sharp left, around 1.7 miles (keep right) to the gate of the coffee plantation. From the botanical garden: circle the park to the south, left after around 2.1 miles, 700 yards to the gate. | **Hours** Viewing only possible by appointment (+95/1/222305) | **Tip** Visit December Farm, around 6 miles from Shan Market (on the NH3 towards Lashio). The park-like farm with ecological cultivation and private petting zoo also contains a restaurant; ice cream, yoghurt, milkshakes and food are all freshly prepared and come highly recommended.

37 Nyaung Done Village
From self-sufficiency to medicinal plants and tourism

The hike from Kalaw to Nyaung Done, a village on a ridge 4,250 feet up that is inhabited predominantly by Palaung, one of the ethnic groups in Shan State that belong to the Mon-Khmer, takes a good two and a half hours. The climb leads through charming valleys, in which traditional rice and vegetable growing is practised with the help of rain collection, and over steep slopes, whose burned areas are evidence of traditional slash-and-burn cultivation as they can still be found all over the mountains of Myanmar.

But on the hike you also see that an enormous transformation is taking place in the mountains: 10 years ago most families lived self-sufficiently, meaning they grew what they needed to live and carried out a little trade in the vicinity. The way on foot to the next city was difficult.

Much has changed today: you now see permanent cropping, namely tea and coffee trees as well as mango, grapefruit, orange and jackfruit trees in large groves. In addition, the cultivation of medicinal plants, such as the castor oil plant, ginger or Chinese cinnamon, is possible at altitude. They are sold, along with tobacco (for the famous Myanmar cheroot cigars) and traditional spice plants, as local specialities on the local and increasingly also on the national market. Some produce even makes it beyond the national border: recently, intermediaries, in particular from China as a result of improved road links, come directly into the villages to buy the harvest and sell it on internationally.

But there are even more new economic activities: the bells from herds of cattle that can be heard when you are out and about herald increasing dairy farming. And the occasional hiking group is a sign of incipient tourism. As of late you can eat and even spend the night in the village as a foreigner. Development projects have helped open up new economic perspectives for the mountain inhabitants.

Address 96°30'8.98" E 20°38'18.59" N | **Getting there** With a guide it is a 6-hour hike from Kalaw through mountainous landscape towards the west. The village is on a mountain ridge. | **Tip** There is a well with washing facilities that was constructed thanks to German donations to be discovered in the centre of the village. Ask about hiking tours at your hotel.

38 Pagoda Mountain
Elevated change in perspective

Not far from the globally famous Inle Lake in the Shan highlands, the urban region of Taunggyi has only begun to gain more attention among international tourists in recent years. After a steep climb of more than 1,300 feet from the level of the lake, you unexpectedly spot Myanmar's fourth-biggest city, located on a narrow plateau running from north to south at 4,750 feet altitude.

Emerging out of the fusion of five small villages and developed in 1894 into the regional administrative centre of the British colonial powers, a hill station, Taunggyi has grown into the most important economic and cultural centre of Shan State. The city, densely populated due to the limited area, offers both the modern-day lively city life with its colourful markets and lots of cultural heritage stretching from pre-colonial religious buildings via the residences of the former Shan princes (Haws) to the private and administrative buildings of the colonial era.

A real change in perspective is offered by the mountain chain to the east of the city, which rises up to 5,710 feet and is called Phaya Mountain (Pagoda Mountain) among locals. Five pagoda locations, all differing greatly in age, building style and view orientation and connected by a road running along the ridge, can be reached by motorbike or car. From the viewpoints of Mya Sein Taung Pagoda in the north, the Dragon Pool Temple in the middle, the large Shwe Pone Pwint Pagoda in the south to the small nameless pagoda in the southeast, views are to be had of both the complete city area as well as the Inle plain in the west and the Shan Hills in the east, up to 6,600 feet tall. A sixth location is on the striking crag that falls away vertically to the city, simply known as The Crag, which can only be reached on foot via a steep path. A breathtaking view of the densely packed buildings in the middle of wooded mountain slopes is worth all the effort of the climb.

Address 97°2'52.29" E 20°46'36.58" N, Taunggyi | Getting there From Myoma Market take Bogyoke Aung San Road to Ye Htwet Oo Street towards the mountain; after about 1.2 miles, cross over the tracks and drive right past a small pagoda; after 160 yards turn sharp right, follow the road uphill for 0.6 miles to the pagoda entrance. Start in the north with Mya Sein Taung Pagoda, all the other locations lie along the mountain road to the south. | Tip The colourful market hustle and bustle in the large Myoma Market and the smaller Market No. 5 (East Circular Road, corner of Nan Thida Street) are worth seeing.

39_ Shan Culture Centre
The language of others

More than 100 young women and men practise traditional Shan dances in the large open square in front of the Shan Literature and Culture Association during the school and semester holidays. You can work out which region in Shan State they come from and which ethnic group they belong to by their colourful costumes and the various headdresses. They practise, for example, the expressive drum dance with the Ozi, a large, mostly black-red-gold-green lacquered or painted frame drum, which are usually around 10 feet long with a diameter of around 24 inches and are elongated in a funnel shape to the ground to form a stand. One very strenuous dance is that of the mythical Kinnara and Kinnari, depicting half-bird, half-human characters; the dancers swing around wide, sweeping wings.

The Shan belong to the Tai-Kadai language family, which comprises around 93 million speakers in Southeast and East Asia (the Thai language of neighbouring Thailand is a subfamily). Linguists distinguish between almost 100 different languages in Myanmar, including main and subgroups, dialects and regiolects. According to estimates, around four to six million people speak Shan in Myanmar. It would be interesting to know more exact figures, as the number of speakers is also connected to the importance of the language group in the educational system.

The aim of the Shan Literature and Culture Association is to foster knowledge about the many various ethnic and language groups, to cultivate their exchange as well as to strengthen Shan culture and language. Traditional and contemporary literature is promoted as well as music. Taunggyi is a very active centre of music production. The various ethnic groups have recently been able to broadcast their own radio programmes. Students from the remote villages of Shan State can also make use of accommodation on the Association's campus.

Address 97°2'22.88" E 20°46'5.7" N, Bogyoke Aung San Road, Taunggyi | Getting there
On Bogyoke Aung San Road towards Hopone to about 330 yards after Shan State Culture
Museum on right side | Hours Mon–Sat 6am–5.30pm, Sun 6am–1pm, closed on national
holidays | Tip A motorbike tour to the diverse viewpoints on Pagoda Mountain with a
detour to the Buddhist University is very appealing.

40__ Shan Breakfast
Hot tofu in a garage

Alongside Mohinga fish soup, Shan noodles are one of the most popular breakfast dishes in Myanmar. The rice noodle varieties, originally from the Shan highlands, are now available across the whole country. The 'hot tofu' (*tofu nway*) version represents a special treat, especially as it is only prepared for breakfast in the street stalls and in garage shops and can, of course, only be eaten freshly prepared.

In the Shan Noodle Shop on East Circular Road in Taunggyi, the big pot of hot tofu mash is already steaming early in the morning. It is made of yellow split peas, Burmese chickpeas, water, turmeric and salt. It is created in a time-consuming process: first the dry pulses are soaked, then pureed in their softened state, and subsequently, after a process of sedimentation, the residual thick mash is slowly cooked with the spices into a creamy consistency.

The hot yellow tofu mash is served on flat, sticky rice noodles (*san see*), garnished with fried, ground garlic (*sichet*), crushed peanuts, chilli powder, herbs (*nan nan pin*) and – depending on the customer's wishes – with chicken curry and Chinese sauce (*kyar nyunt*). The whole thing is mixed together vigorously with chopsticks and long golden-brown deep-fried dumpling sticks (*e kya kway*), which are cut into pieces and served with it, are dipped gleefully in the sauce.

It is a special delight to experience this particular kind of Shan noodles in a nice atmosphere with friendly conversation in a full garage shop. Getting up early is essential: hot tofu is only for breakfast as the tofu mash turns hard after two or three hours of cooking.

Lately, *tofu nway* is also available in some special Shan noodle restaurants in the big cities at lunchtime, but not always. It is definitely worth asking for it.

Address 97°2'24.43" E 20°47'45.33" N, Yae Aye Kwin Ward, East Circular Road, Taunggyi | **Getting there** 440 yards north of Market No. 5, first shop, northwest corner of the street crossing | **Hours** Breakfast only | **Tip** A hiking tour to the striking rock formation on Pagoda Mountain, the Crag, offers a grandiose view of the colonial administrative quarter. Beware hikers with vertigo: there are no railings on the precipice by the pagoda.

41__Pioneer Wine

German wine artistry

Those of the opinion that no palatable wine can be produced in the tropics should be prepared to learn better at the Ayetharyar vineyard. The estate, owned by a businessman from Saarland, Bert Morsbach, and run by the German cellar master Hans Leiendecker, has since 1997 produced white, red and rosé wines, which even to Western palates compare favourably with middle European wines. Around 200,000 to 300,000 bottles are sold annually under the Aythaya designation. The wines can be tasted and bought on site, but are also on offer in supermarkets in Myanmar's big cities. The first 3,000 saplings were imported from Central Europe, but now they are self-sufficient in seedlings.

The vineyard sees itself as the supporter of an agricultural innovation. In order to utilise the full capacity of the winery, for which their own fruit do not yet suffice, grapes from neighbouring wine-growers are bought, which, for their part, have been inaugurated in the fundamentals of cultivation and harvesting. The grape varieties Shiraz and Sauvignon dominate, forming the main component in the cuvées of the red, rosé and white wines offered. Beyond these wines, the experimental verve of the cellar master first put a dessert wine and a high-proof on the market, then a grappa made of muscat grapes and a lychee fruit brandy. The next expansion of the range was their own rosé, sparkling wine.

The vineyard is linked to a comprehensive and continually growing touristic offer. Tours of the operation present the whole chain of production, from the breeding of saplings via the cultivation to the management of the cellar and bar. The vineyard is also home to a restaurant, which people like to visit from neighbouring Taunggyi or from Inle Lake, especially in the evening for a sunset dinner. The Monte di Vino Lodge offers classy accommodation with its bungalows downhill from the winery.

Address 97°0'58.5" E 20°47'21.5" N, Ayetharyar, www.myanmar-vineyard.com | Getting
there On the NH4 (Bogyoke Aung San Road), beyond the east exit of town, around a
sharp corner on the ascent to the city of Taunggyi located 800 feet higher | Tip How about
not only telling your guests at home about your trip to Myanmar by means of images and
video clips, but actually giving them a taste of it with a rare bottle of wine?

42 Inndein

Bamboo forests flooded with tourism

Children play in a stream surrounded by dams; not far off, women wash the laundry, men their motorbikes (and sometimes it is the other way round); livestock is watered, elsewhere drinking water is extracted. The inhabitants of the village congregate here in the late afternoon, to meet, greet and share news. And bamboo grows all over, as tall as houses. A real bamboo forest, silvery light and fine green. And rustling in the wind, but with an unusual noise, as the leaves scrape against each other.

We know all kinds of bamboo plants, tall and short, from the garden or balcony: a touch of the exotic, but rampant and often very difficult to control. In large areas of Myanmar you will find bamboo by the forest. Bamboo is actually a grass. It belongs to the sweet grass family; there are more than 1,000 different kinds of bamboo worldwide. As the plants are able to cope with great aridity as well as with large quantities of rain or poor soil, and neither heat nor cold is able to harm them, they can be found pretty much anywhere. Rapidly growing, straight as a die, bamboo is a blessing for the rural population. Without it, living and working in the village would barely be possible – bamboo groves are like a practical DIY store just next door. (Almost) nothing works without bamboo: it is a building material for everything and everyone. Cheap, light, practical, always available. Bamboo canes are easy to slash with slashers and saws. It is also easy to transport and connect, install, bend, mortise, flatten – for floors, walls, doors, ceilings and roofs. You can eat bamboo, and drink out of it. The observant traveller will find evidence of its endless range of uses in people's everyday life all over. Travel guides point to Inndein for its ruins, temples, souvenir shops and tourist attractions. Less obvious is the connection between nature and everyday life that emerges. Sometimes you get the impression that many don't see the woods for the attractions.

Address 96°50'16.06" E 20°27'34.53" N | Getting there By boat from Nyaung Shwe to Inndein, cross the river south of the market, follow the pagoda ascent for around 440 yards, then cross the monastery grounds north of the stairs to the bamboo forest | Tip At the end of the ascent to Shwe Inndein Pagoda is a pagoda field with a beautiful view of the Inle Lake landscape from the hill to its south.

43_ The Haw
Who still knows it exists?

They are no longer as numerous and seem hardly to exist to tourists. Many of the proud palaces of the once more than 40 Shan principalities, the so-called *haw*, have been destroyed over the last 80 years by war, fire or for political reasons. The rulers of the states (*saopha*), the tax-paying states (*myosa*) and other smaller territories (*ngwegunmhu*) shaped the history of east Myanmar for over 800 years. As allied states, they were able to extend their power right up to Upper Burma into the 16th century. Changing alliances and neighbours growing in strength led to a weakening of their power, but never to a loss of their autonomy – not even under British colonial rule. Feudal rule was only ended through the destabilisation process after independence in 1948 and after the transfer of all princely rights to the central government in 1962. Despite still owning houses and estates, many Saophas went into exile.

With its 28 square miles, Nawng Mawn was one of the smallest Myosa-run states – in existence since 1602, it merged with the larger neighbouring area of Mongpawn in 1931. Hardly known to anyone anymore, the *haw* is to be found in the old city of Myo Haung, around 31 miles southeast of Taunggyi in a rice-growing area of the Nam Tamphak valley.

More interesting than the 20th-century *haw*, today a Buddhist monastery, and the more than 1,000-year-old pagoda, is the almost 0.4-square-mile village, with embankments on the east side and water ditches on the west. It is assumed that this is evidence of a weir system that is unusual for this region, but there's a lack of well-founded information. The lively village life gives hope that the historic heritage will be preserved, but the overgrown Myosa graves in the northeast of the site and the systematic and ever-closer reallocation of the surrounding farmland indicate the danger of cultural heritage being lost.

Address 97°11'40.31" E 20°32'01.28" N, Nawng Mawn | **Getting there** From Taunggyi around 13 miles on the NH4 to Hopone, then turn right onto the NH5, follow the road 20.5 miles to Nawng Mawn; in the village right after the school complex take the road to the right to the old village, around 1 mile through rice paddies and habitation | **Tip** Visit two wonderful viewpoints west of Hopone: at a crossroads around 5 miles east of Taunggyi's new industrial park, just in front of the tollbooth before you reach Hopone, either turn left to a small pagoda on a hill or right for a short mountain hike.

44_ Cave Monastery

I have a dream …

A young monk of the Pa-O had a dream: he saw how the members of the Pa-O found protection and refuge during times of war and conflict in the large cave systems of the surrounding karst mountains, setting themselves up there for a longer period and living out a difficult existence. He dreamt that the soldiers, volunteers and deputies would hole up in the caves and would fear for their lives – and some would only survive because they knew their way around in the labyrinth of the caves, underground passages and rivers. The monk was particularly attracted to one of the biggest caves, Htan Sann Cave. It appeared to him in a dream, and he resolved to convert it into a subterranean monastery, so that conflicts could never again be fought there. The dream of reconciliation between the ethnic groups was to be given a home. The underground monastery has since become a reality. Strictly guarded until just a few years ago, foreigners can now visit with special permission.

A vast cave system awaits. It is around one mile long, but not very deep, so that you can walk at ground level for the most part – barefoot of course, as you are in a monastery after all. Fresh winds frequently blow through the underground passages and "halls" – there are openings somewhere up high. Once you have become accustomed to the darkness, you can see bats on the roof of some parts of the cave.

Buddha figures have been installed in prominent places, under white or beige-brown stalactite garlands, and also pagodas, colourfully decorated, partly adorned with blinking lights. There are figurative representations of wild animals, which symbolise the primitiveness of the site. A huge stalactite dome is impressively lit, immersed in deep silence, in which (if the visitors are quiet) only the gurgling of the small stream and the dripping of falling water droplets can be heard, in a magical half-sphere of light. Several beautiful, tranquil pools lie in recesses, their edges adorned by bright white sinter terraces.

Address 97°20'8.9" E 20°49'8.17" N, Htan Sann Cave | Getting there Around 25 miles east of Taunggyi; from Taunggyi to Hopone on the NH4, pass through Hopone, car park and access to the cave are around 0.6 miles beyond the driveway to Htam Sann Pagoda and Religious Hall | Hours All day, admission to the cave for foreigners US$20 | Tip The festival of lights with flying lanterns in Hopone is not as big and less hectic than the Taunggyi balloon festival.

45__Border Trading Paradise
Entering a casino with a visa

Tachileik on the Myanmar side and Mae Sai on the Thailand side of the border – within a few years two sleepy towns became a booming double city in the 'Golden Triangle' border area between Myanmar, Thailand and Laos. The Mae Nam Sai River separates the two linked parts from each other.

Since 28 August, 2013, it has been possible for foreigners with valid entry visas to cross the border on the overland route normally – a sensation at the time. This process of opening up 'in small' saw the investment and trade ties between the two countries strengthen sharply. While you can buy agricultural products from Myanmar in Tachileik as well as cheap mass-produced goods from China, including counterfeit Western-branded goods, household appliances and electronic devices in the shops and market stalls, on the Thai side seeds for growing vegetables in higher altitudes, candied fruit, dried fruit and furniture for the steadily growing number of new households are on offer. Cross-border tourism is also growing: those in need of some change can try their luck in one of the three casinos in the border region, and it is still possible to get an easy visa extension for Thailand. In recent years, numerous new hotels have popped up in the border region. The first large tourist groups from southern China reach the border city over a new bridge over the Mekong in northern Thailand.

Other things are of greater importance for the local population: many inhabitants of Tachileik commute daily, for weeks or months, to work in Thailand, where the wages are considerably higher than in Myanmar. The pay gap also has a positive effect for Thailand: labour from Myanmar is employed in construction and road building, in agriculture, industrial production and the service sector. They work in housekeeping, in warehouses and logistics, as cleaning staff and in tourism – seasonally, as they can be sent back home at the end of the season.

Address 99°53'4.79" E 20°27'0.37" N, Tachileik | Getting there Airplane to Tachileik or Kengtung (around 98 miles north of Tachileik) as road link from Taunggyi not open to foreigners | Tip It is interesting to watch the numerous travel groups from Thailand, who drive into 'exotic' Myanmar to 'go shopping'.

46_Mobye Reservoir

Energy for the country as far as the eye can see

Mains supply electricity is one of those things in Myanmar ... Even in the big cities you can't expect to plug in and play all the time. A cosy evening in front of the television, or a hot cup of tea on a cold winter morning in the mountains? Can't be guaranteed. Here you have to plan for a lack of electricity. Everyone in the country knows the situation: to this day – and apart from in a few enclaves – the supply is scarce, the availability unpredictable. Electricity is in especially short supply and unpredictable in the hot dry season, if the hydroelectric power plants don't have enough water. Sometimes electricity can be in scarce supply for a few hours.

But Myanmar's energy sector is developing rapidly: the installed energy capacities have been extended from almost 1,000 megawatts in 2000 to almost 4,000 today, of which more than two-thirds come from the 30 hydroelectric power plants. But for the general population it is difficult: a large amount of the energy goes to neighbouring countries – after all, they financed the majority of the plants. Furthermore, most reservoirs also serve as water reserves for irrigation purposes and for flood control.

As part of the reparation payments after World War II, the Japanese built the now more than 60-year-old hydroelectric power plant Baluchaung No. 2 (also known as the Lawpita Hydropower Project), one of the oldest and most reliable power plants in Myanmar, which is supposed to cover up to 25 per cent of the annual energy needs of the country. The Mobye reservoir on the Balu Chaung River is the large reservoir for this and another hydroelectric power plant. You can get close to the banks in Pekon and sense the dimensions of this gigantic reservoir when you let your gaze travel as far as it can go, and take in the play of light and the apparent merger of the water with the sky. Yet there are still some villages right next to the reservoir that aren't connected to the electrical grid.

Address 97°1'35.86" E 19°51'1.56" N, Pekon | **Getting there** From Kalaw on the NH54 around 80 miles southwards to Pekon, or fly to Loikaw, from there around 25 miles on the NH5 first northwards then, after around 7 miles, turn left towards Pekon, or take a six-hour boat trip from Nyaung Shwe via Inle Lake and Moebyel Lake to Pekon | **Tip** A boat trip on Moebyel Lake from Pekon is beautiful.

47 __ Loikaw Clock Tower

He who rings the bell

Clock towers are almost everywhere, and were very important in the past. The British introduced them as a new element, a building for time. Until then, the emphasis had been on timelessness, not to mention eternity, as temples and pagodas embody it – as symbols of the eternal, the ultimate. Suddenly time counted. The British left their mark – literally. And they introduced a new standard: a city should always have a clock tower. A village didn't warrant one. The clock tower was a sign of specialness, privilege. The clock tower is thus the established landmark of urbanity. And clock towers mark the centre of a city; they are to this day central landmarks, lighthouses, also for spatial orientation. The clocks followed bells as acoustic signals, and then came the loudspeaker. They were and are easy to install – and they reach the people, with everything that needs to be communicated. In many cities the clock tower is a common meeting place for rendevous.

As a traveller, you won't necessarily notice them directly. A part of the charm in Myanmar as a holiday destination is that by no means does everything run according to plan. Yet take note: people in Myanmar are in fact punctual. Being punctual is a virtue and a duty for everyone. One doesn't necessarily need a clock tower for that. And yet they are still paid attention to, and new ones are built.

The clock tower in Loikaw is relatively new, unlike in numerous cities in Myanmar where the clock towers date back to the British era. It was built in the late 1960s. With an architectural modern-dynamic design, it is almost dainty and playful, colourful, striking, confident, with technical appeal and a globe on the spire. Effort was made to lend the design an independent, artistic signature. The architect felt it worthy of that. Innovation in flux. He who rings the bell, sets the standard. That still applies today.

Address 97°12'42.89" E 19°40'37.73" N, Loikaw | Getting there Near Myo Nan Pagoda beside NH5, not far from Ba Lu Chaung River | Tip There are picturesque houses on the east bank of the Ba Lu Chaung, north of the large bridge over the river at Thirimingalar Market.

48 Prayer Mountain

374 steps to the summit

In other areas of Myanmar you see mountains and smaller hills crowned by pagodas that you might laboriously climb up to, but after reaching them you feel relieved. On the outskirts of Thandaung Gyi, this model has been adopted by Christianity: around a dozen small chapels line the ascent to a viewing platform and the largest chapel on the summit. The chapels are donations by individual families, who in this way commemorate their parents, grandparents or other relatives and, as on a pilgrim trail, grant an insight into a small piece of their respective family histories. At the same time they emphasise the fact that a considerable portion of the Kayin (Karen) are adherents to Christianity; they are predominantly Baptists, but also Anglicans, Catholics or members of Pentecostal churches. The chapels thus also document the waves of missionary activity that covered several areas of Upper Burma under British colonial rule and led to the spread of Christianity.

The architecture of the chapels is quite varied: there are the simple little rectangular chapels, in which half a dozen people would struggle to fit; there is the larger chapel that crowns the peak, in front of which a small triangular platform spreads out like the deck over a ship's bow; and the chapels whose side walls are based on praying hands. The colours white and red define all of the buildings and the well-secured path that leads up past the chapels, whose 374 steps (as is stated at the bottom) can be climbed without effort.

From the platform you have two views. On one side, it is of the subdivided town of Thandaung Gyi with its small market and school centre, many churches, the investment ruins of an unfinished tourist resort and the residential houses built on the slopes. On the other lie the seemingly almost untouched mountain ranges, covered in subtropical forest and sparsely populated with many very small villages.

Address 96°41'13.29" E 19°4'46.12" N, Thandaung Gyi | Getting there From Taungoo on the NH5 eastwards, after around 13 miles turn left onto the regional road to Thandaung Gyi, around 12 miles to the central square, from here around 1.8 miles (45 minutes) on foot uphill to Naw Bu Baw Prayer Mountain | Tip You can get a good view of Prayer Mountain and most of its chapels from the hill directly opposite, on which several chapels have also been built.

49_Old Tea Factory

Reading the tea leaves

Thandaung Gyi was organised as a hill station in the British colonial era: one could escape here, at around 3,950 feet above sea level, when the heat in Taungoo in the lowlands became unbearable. The British also brought economic innovations with them. Among these was the cultivation of tea, with which they had gathered great experience both in India and on the Malaysian peninsula. The slopes next to the town are still covered in narrow terraces today, which trace the relief like contour lines and are planted with tea bushes. A tea factory was built on the hill over the town in the building of the colonial-era secondary school to prepare and process the pickings.

In the course of Myanmar's independence and the civil wars, Thandaung Gyi's tea culture deteriorated. The tea bushes were no longer cultivated or were replaced, and the tea factory also seemed to have given way to disrepair. The tea factory machinery survived, even though it is rarely used. But age plays no role. In the last few years the situation has changed: in town, small areas for the cultivation of tea bushes have emerged; the terraces are better maintained again and some already exhibit new seedlings. In the tea factory the machines that are set up for rolling, fermenting, cutting and further steps in the process make a well-kept impression, and the building, imposing in such a small town, has just been repainted. Here an old tradition is being revived.

This fits in with an agricultural policy that is increasingly banking on regional potential. The area around Thandaung Gyi is not only known for tea cultivation, but also for the growing of the cardamom plant, a relative of ginger. The coveted spice, which is one of the most expensive spices alongside saffron and real vanilla, is obtained from the hand-picked capsules containing the seeds, which are crushed or ground. Today, the largest proportion of the cardamom grown in Myanmar is sold via China.

Address 96°40'27.62" E 19°4'16.29" N, Thandaung Gyi| | Getting there Short walk to the building around 330 yards north of the central square | Tip Visit the Hindu shrine on the way there that reminds us that as a British colony, Burma/Myanmar was subordinate to Indian administration and that the Nepalese Gurkha enjoyed special esteem among the Indian troops.

50_ San Su Si
No Prussian reminiscence

In 2002, on the edge of one of the hills of Thandaung Gyi, 'San Su Si' (as the plaque by the entrance states), a Christian community centre that also offers guests accommodation and meals, was founded. The idea and the donation for the construction of the building apparently came from a German who liked Sanssouci Palace, but documents and detailed knowledge of this have disappeared over the years. On the ground floor there is an assembly room as well as four double rooms, while upstairs a dormitory is available. A small, frugal travel group can be accommodated easily. Don't expect luxury, however. The two-bed rooms are plain, the washrooms and toilets unpretentious but clean. But you will be able to sleep in peace without being disturbed by passing cars – until around 4am when the first crow of a cockerel punctually announces the dawning of a new day. The attendants of the facility always do their best to make their guests comfortable and conjure up all of the meals in the neighbouring wooden house.

San Su Si stands for the tentative beginnings, since the end of the ethnic conflicts after 2012, to establish local and pilgrim tourism in a place that is organised by the community itself and creates earning opportunities for the population alongside agriculture and trade. Since, several accommodations and small restaurants have sprung up through private or church initiatives. There is no doubt that the whole town benefits from this new economic focus.

If you walk down the street from San Su Si and turn off to the left into an alley, climbing to the top of the small hill you will get to another unexpected sight. The mighty building of the former colonial-era prison, nowadays a large assembly room of the Christians of Thandaung Gyi, covered in the algae and moss of the 'tropical finish', offers a beautiful view of the hills around the small town covered in tea bushes.

Address 96°40'16.41" E 19°3'57.84" N, Thandaung Gyi | Getting there 440-yard walk downhill from central square, at sharp left curve go straight uphill, around 220 yards to reach the building | Tip From the middle of town you can take a walk through the tea planting areas (beware: there is danger of snakes!).

51__Glass Noodle Maker

Noodles on a washing line

On the way from Taungoo to Thandaung Gyi you may see what seems like laundry hanging up to dry in an inconspicuous garden. If you take a closer look, the supposed textiles turn out to be long, thin strips, that – laid over slats – are indeed hung to dry. The material they are made of, however, is rice.

Rice noodles are often also referred to as cellophane or glass noodles, because unlike noodles made of durum wheat, they appear to be transparent. The garden in which they are hung up to dry belongs to a small operation that produces these glass noodles from rice with little effort. The factory is more of a medium-sized craftsman's workshop. The production process has a very short value-added chain: sacks of rice, just as they are when they come from the threshing floors near the fields, going first to more central warehouses and then into general sale, are stored in a large shed. The second raw material is simply water, in which rice is blended like in a mortar mix machine, but not into the grainy rice that is served in every restaurant in Myanmar, rather to a viscous mash. This is done mainly by family members, but also a few workers from the neighbourhood, following the principle of the meat mincer, mechanically being pressed through a mould disc with around two dozen holes, from which the half-finished noodles already ooze. They are pre-dried in the production hall, cut into about five-feet-long strips, then brought outside and laid over the long slats there, in order to continue drying and in the process also bleach.

If all of the slats are occupied, the noodles are spread out on the floor on plastic foil. The tropical warmth of the dry season ensures that the noodles are portioned and packed after a short time – just the way they then appear in the shops. The small factory has its own label and the noodles are sold through an intermediary who in turn supplies the shops.

Address 96°27'27.86" E 18°56'44.37" N | Getting there From Taungoo to Thandaung Gyi on the NH5, around 0.8 miles after the bridge over the Sittaung the courtyard entrance is on the right side after a small pagoda | Tip Feeling lively? How about a visit to the Pho Kyar elephant camp around 40 miles northeast of Taungoo (4 miles from the Yangon-Mandalay Highway eastwards in the Bago mountains). Elephant rides, bathing and a visit to an Oozy village (elephant drivers) are on offer.

52__Taungoo Moat
All-round protection and enclosed royal lake

Going all the way around on foot, roughly six miles, will take you a while. But you can walk without a problem around the old, completely preserved city fortifications, with a wide moat and a high earth wall with a masonry core. In the dry season you may struggle to identify the moat, as it is largely silted up and full of water hyacinths and pondweed, but in the rainy season you can see it in its functional state. The city wall also takes some searching for, as it is largely covered with soil and overgrown by bushes and trees. The wall and surroundings are mostly inaccessible. Near the west gate, a piece of the wall has been laid bare and is walkable; nearby there is also a private museum with archaeological finds.

The history of Taungoo begins in 1191, when King Narapadisithu, on a trip to Shwedagon Pagoda, found three pagodas overgrown with trees, which were from the time when Buddhism spread through today's Myanmar under Emperor Ashoka. Much later Taungoonge (the 'little Taungoo') was founded nearby and in 1279 the city Danyawaddy was established, from which 28 kings ruled. In 1485, King Mingyinyo mounted the throne and founded the new capital Ketumadi, today's Taungoo, in 1510. Monasteries and pagodas were constructed in all four corners within the quadratic city complex and a large natural lake in the southwest corner was made even larger.

The city has been destroyed, relocated and restored again several times over. The royal lake, Kandawgyi, enabled its defence on several occasions, and King Bayint Naung also took four months to capture the city in 1550. Until the recent past, the lake served the people for extracting drinking water, for bathing and for fishing. When a large hotel was built directly on its shore in 2005, the owner had the lake fenced in. You can now walk around the shore for pleasure at fixed opening hours.

Address 96°25'9.15" E 18°57'10.58" N, Taungoo | Getting there Northwest corner of the old city at the connecting road to Yangon-Mandalay Expressway | Hours Sunrise to sunset | Tip The 'elephant house' at the northeast corner of Shwe Sandaw Pagoda is named after the two elephant figures in front of the derelict former palace-like building of a monastery.

53 Bazaar on the Steps

Health kick of a different kind

Only a hair of Buddha keeps the seemingly free-floating Golden Rock, one of the most important religious sites in the country, in balance. A stream of around three million mainly domestic pilgrims a year on the narrow, 3,600-foot-high crest of Mount Kyaikhtio, is the cause of a unique conglomerate of cult buildings, guesthouses, restaurants and markets including the workshops and living spaces of the shop owners.

In the markets that cling to the steep slopes up to the Golden Rock and in the northern section of the pagoda grounds there is a thriving trade in wild-animal body parts and drugs of traditional medicine. Several hundred shops offer whole carcasses and body parts such as skulls, paws, soles of elephant feet, teeth, antlers, fur, skins and scales and processed bones, but especially aromatic oils, salves and pastes. Nearly everyone solicits custom with a large cauldron, in which oil and bodily fluids, from an individual composition of serow head and forelegs, macaque skull, dried python, centipedes and much more, are collected in a process lasting several weeks and bottled using scented pieces of wood. These oils and salves are used to treat joint and muscle pain, headaches, skin disorders, broken bones, cataracts, nose bleeds and swelling.

A clear 'no photos!' shows the ambivalence towards this trade. Although the national legislative instruments are devised for the protection of wild animals and the legal use of traditional medicine, there are loopholes in the law. Local hunter-dealer networks, lack of awareness in the general population, local poverty, insufficient modern healthcare provision and a growing demand from Asia join the difficult enforcement of the law to allow these markets to exist, but there have been recent improvements. Openly presented animal carcasses are becoming rare and are being replaced by herbs, dried fruits and roots as well as the assortment of bottles of tincture with their pungent smells.

Address 97°5'52.19" E 17°29'1.91" N, Kyaikhtio | Getting there By truck from Kin Pun Sakhan (around 10 miles northeast of Kyaikto), 9 miles on a mountain road to the hill station, then by foot around 930 yards to the pagoda platform; cross the platform to the northwest corner and the entrance to the bazaar on the steps | Hours Entry into 'Kyaikhtiyo Archaeological Zone' costs 6,000 kyat (valid for two days). | Tip Sunset/sunrise on the Golden Rock is uniquely atmospheric. Around the full moon it can get pretty busy, when up to 10,000 Myanmarese spend the night on the mountain.

54 Myathabeik Pagoda

Karst and sea

Thaton, the former centre of the Mon kingdom, is perhaps not the kind of place you'd like to spend a lot of time, but it is worth making a proper stop on the way to Mawlamyine or Hpa-an. There isn't much left to make out of its earlier importance, when Thaton developed into a trading base between India and Southeast Asia and claimed the title 'Suvannabhum(i)' – golden land. The sedimentation on the coast has made the former seaside location into an interior site, 10 miles from the coast. The fortification was largely destroyed after the conquest by King Anawratha in 1057. The British revived the trading centre again. Today, the town is a stop-off for traffic and trade between Bago and Mawlamyine, a small town between the coastal plain and the mountains, via which the Thanlwin valley is reached. A clock tower watches over the central junction, and the Shwezaryan Pagoda is close by. The city also contains a few handsome houses from the British colonial era that are still well preserved.

Away from the hustle and bustle along the main road, at the end of a small side street, begins the climb to Myathabeik Pagoda. The covered and thus shaded stairway makes the ascent easy. After every few steps is a ledge with a cemented bench; traders offer refreshments. Every hundredth step is marked with a number. After 904 steps the destination is reached, and the pagoda platform offers a magnificent view. To the west are the coastal plains, intensively planted with rice and fruit trees; to the east the mountains open up so much that you get an insight into the wooded backdrop that accompanies the way south. Numerous protrusions on the rim of the mountain are occupied by pagodas or stupas that gleam in the sun like milestones. What appears to be a special feature during the climb, repeats in a highly impressive way and imparts the feeling of a rich cultural landscape. Here you can sense why Myanmar is so often described as the golden land.

55_ Over the Thanlwin

Longest wonder-bridge in Myanmar

A structure that deserves attention can be admired from the river-side promenade of Mawlamyine. Although not the largest bridge in Southeast Asia, by a long way, it is at least the longest bridge in Myanmar that is open to road and (single-track) rail traffic as well as pedestrians. Mawlamyine, called Moulmein during British colonial rule, can hope to regain some of its former economic importance as the sixth-biggest city in Myanmar with this connection to the national transport network.

The second-biggest river in Myanmar, the Thanlwin (also Salween), flows into the Gulf of Mottama (Martaban) of the Andaman Sea here in the city. An average of around 400 billion cubic metres of water flow into the sea here annually, though with enormous fluctuations between the runoff-rich monsoon season and the outflow-poor dry months. Spanning the wide estuary, which assumes very varying dimensions under the influence of the seasons, was an engineering challenge. The bridge has spanned the around 2.2-mile-wide estuary since 2005. It is important to understand the political and developmental significance: beforehand it was difficult to reach the south of Myanmar, which was cut off time and again because the train ended in Mottama and there was only a ferry service or shipping. The bridge makes a continuous connection for accessibility to the narrow but important strip of coast to Kawthoung in the far south possible. Furthermore, the bridge, as an expansion of Asian Highway Number 1, makes access to Thailand, which continually grows in importance as a neighbouring trade partner, easier. However, road traffic in Mawlamyine has increased noticeably as a result. In 2006 the bridge was also opened up to rail traffic after a process requiring the building of access ramps – 1.4 miles long on the north side and 1.22 miles long on the south side. Yangon can now be reached directly in nine to ten hours.

Address 97°37'5.07" E 16°30'39.71" N | **Getting there** On the NH8 from Mottama over the Thanlwin/Salween River to Mawlamyine | **Tip** There's an impressive view of the bridge from the terrace of the Attran Hotel, and the garden restaurant serves good food.

56 Surtee Sunni Jamae Mosque
Out of India

Between 1826 and 1852, when Mawlamyine became British Burma's first capital, the British expanded the city for the numerous new arrivals. While a good 18,000 inhabitants lived here in 1830, the number grew rapidly and reached around 60,000 people only 70 years later. The exploitation of rich resources, especially teak and rice, attracted immigrants from all around the world. Mawlamyine developed into a centre of ship building and rice mills. The city was characterised as 'Little England' or 'Little London' at the time. In his world-famous poem 'The Road to Mandalay', Rudyard Kipling mentions the old Moulmein (as today's Mawlamyine was called at the time) Pagoda. From here, today's Kayak Than Lan Pagoda, a fantastic view opens up over the city and the Thanlwin.

There are still rich architectural testimonies to this past to be found in Mawlamyine to this day. St Patrick's Cathedral, for example, founded by the De La Salle brothers in 1829; the prison, built in 1908 and probably the location of George Orwell's short story 'A Hanging'; and numerous colonial administration and residential buildings, often adorned with stylistic elements that are remotely reminiscent of Renaissance and baroque façades. Among the mosques, the Surtee Sunni Jamae Mosque, built from 1846 to 1848 for the Muslim officers and civil servants in British service, is one of the most important.

The British summoned hundreds of thousands of Indians to Burma, especially colonial officers and labourers. Furthermore, countless merchants used the favour of the British to do business – they all naturally preferred to establish themselves in the cities. Numerous Hindu temples and mosques were built for them and by them in the subsequent period, so that Moulmein became more and more a city dominated numerically by Indians.

Address 97°37'6.15" E 16°29'28.4" N, Surtee Sunni Jamae Mosque, Lower Main Road, Mawlamyine | **Getting there** Around 330 yards south of the central market on the right side of Lower Main Road | **Hours** All day | **Tip** A very special moment can be experienced at sunset on the Khaik Than Lan Pagoda, when mantras ring out from the loudspeakers installed all over. Unfortunately they are not sung regularly, but they will enhance the already wonderful atmosphere if you do chance to hear them.

57 Colonial-style University
Educated relic

Among the many public institutions that the British established towards the end of their roughly 125-year-long history of colonialism were those of higher education – colleges and universities. A college affiliated with the University of Calcutta had existed since 1878, but the University of Yangon was founded in 1920 as the country's first own university; the University of Mandalay followed as the second in 1925. Establishing any more did not seem necessary for a long time, as the few members of the academic elite preferred to go to Great Britain to study, and the political priority was the not long-term promotion of education. It wasn't until 1953 that the third institution followed: Mawlamyine, founded as Moulmein Intermediate College, upgraded to Mawlamyaing Degree College in 1964, finally obtaining university status in 1986.

'Old' university therefore seems a little hyperbolic, but is right because the present location of Mawlamyine University is on the eastern edge of the city beyond the mountain range, in a large, beautifully designed campus area with appealing landscape. The building, recreated in the British style in terms of architecture and style, seems a little neglected structurally – no wonder, in light of the enormous amount of monsoonal precipitation and numerous tropical storms in the last decades. The buildings of the North Campus are noteworthy because they mark a presence within the city – unlike other university campuses that normally lie outside the urban area. If you stroll around the site, you will discover an appealing, typical teaching and learning atmosphere and lively culture of revision. Universities in Myanmar are evermore present in public perception, not only for the acquisition of education and certificates. The number of students is constantly growing, also because parents now earn and invest more. What's more, they are increasingly international. This is such a place.

Address 97°37'30.58" E 16°29'10.82" N, Upper Main Road, Mawlamyine | Getting there From central market take the Lower Main Road south past the large mosque; after around 440 yards turn left into Ye Baw Gone Street to the roundabout on Upper Main Road, turn right and walk around 500 yards to the access at St Patrick's Church on the left | Tip There are some very pretty parks on Upper Main Road, as well as colonial churches, for example St Matthew's Church (Upper Main Road/U Zina Phayar Street).

58_ Waterside Promenade

Punctual seagulls in formation

On the estuary of the Thanlwin/Salween, the country's second-biggest river, lies the old Mon city of Mawlamyine, which was later even the capital of British India for quarter of a century. The city has maintained its colonial charm in many streets. It is bustling and lively near the various markets of the city, but quiet and serene away from this hive of activity.

It is easy to forget that the city is one of the largest in the country, after Yangon, Mandalay, Taunggyi and Nay Pyi Taw. The multitude of urban cultural heritage sites, whether it be the monasteries and pagodas on the mountain, the colonial houses or several churches and mosques, make a leisurely stroll through the streets a must. Particularly pretty are the sunsets over the island to the west, Bilu Kyun, also known as Ogre Island, which are best admired from the elevated Kyeik Than Lan Pagoda.

This is also the time of day that the Strand Road north of Myoma Market comes to life. Families with children, lovers and teenagers on their mopeds populate the waterside promenade in order to experience a special spectacle. Just in time for sunset, seagulls in expectation of feeding fly in flocks from north to south along the promenade and skilfully catch the dried rice balls thrown for them. Flying in a large loop, they repeat this spectacle until the sun has set. The flying skills of the birds are impressive, as despite high speeds, together with the swerves needed to catch the food, there aren't any collisions between the animals. Even spontaneously held out arms or selfie sticks protruded into their flight paths only cause brief discord in the eternal stream of seagulls flying past. Snack- and drink-sellers round off the evening event, which becomes a lovely, entertaining experience in combination with the sunset, the light flow of air from the flapping of the gulls and the sea breeze in this tropical environment.

Address 97°37'5.16" E 16°29'51.54" N, Strand Road, Mawlamyine | Getting there Promenade by Strand Hotel | Hours The spectacle begins between 5 and 5.30pm and continues until the sun has set. | Tip A tour through the various markets is a good way to spend the day: Central Market, New Market (tobacco and spices), the vegetable and meat market by the stadium, the small street market north of the prison and Thanlwin Market (fish) on Lower Main Road at the corner of the southern Strand Road.

59_ Ywalut Village

Pipes for the world

'Mr Meier from Germany had the idea. I gave him one as a present and he said that it would be easier to transport if you could screw off the bowl.' The talk is of a long pipe with a proud projecting tobacco bowl. The story is told with an endearing smile by the owner of the workshop, where in particular pipes and walking sticks, wooden vases and now and then elephant tusks are carved – out of wood of course – when a customer orders them.

An arduous journey must be made in order to reach it, taking the ferry from the mainland onto the island, then motorbike taxi to the village. The trip takes two hours from Mawlamyine. In a family house with associated workshop in the middle of Ywalut village, a father and son work with simple tools, lately with the addition of some supporting technology for the woodturning. The clean, neat workshop conveys an impression of artisan professionalism and dedication.

High-quality handmade goods are produced here, now already in the fourth generation. Some pipe bowls portray tigers, dragons or a peacock; others, upon request, depict famous personalities. The products of the work are sold to Mandalay and Taunggyi, and sometimes exported to Germany, India, China, Thailand, Taiwan and Saudi Arabia – indirectly via facilitating merchants. The owner also has a long path behind him: a craftsman, an artist, can survive on the periphery if he is well connected.

The island is forecast a big future: a bridge and an industrial area are in planning stages. That is good news for the family business: 'Many tourists will visit us. Sometimes they come just to watch and ask if they should pay something for it. But I don't want that. Because the government said: "Please warmly help the tourists." They spend lots of money to come to us, so I want to help to make sure everything is pleasant for them.' He means exactly what he says.

Address 97°30'51.29" E 16°26'7.3" N, Thain Pan Ward, Ma Kinn Street, No. 55, Ywalut | Getting there Ferry from the promenade, then motorbike taxi to Ywalut. The bridge to the island was opened very recently, so now Ywalut can also be reached by car. | Tip You can observe the production of slates along the way to Ywalut.

60 Zwegabin Mountain
A view to sweat for

You are welcomed to Lumbini Buddha Garden by hundreds of larger-than-life Buddha statues, arranged in many long rows in a somewhat overgrown ambience. From the car park, next to which there are also some simple restaurants, begins a strenuous climb up a path, which is largely laid out as steps, but represents a certain challenge because of the uneven heights of the steps. After about a quarter of the way it is possible to take a rest next to a monastery complex, and then, before the beginning of the last quarter, there is another informal sales stand, where refreshing drinks and crisps are sold. Those who have time should use both resting places in order also to observe the passing visitors. The climb is clearly fun, especially for many young people. A simple restaurant represents a semblance of tourist infrastructure on the summit.

The 2,369-foot-tall Zwegabin Mountain is made of limestone. Just like the steeply looming mountains of the neighbourhood, it is a product of tropical weathering, which has created jagged, inaccessible-seeming rock formations partly covered by lush vegetation. The monastery with its ancillary facilities on the summit may have arisen on a remote and hard-to-reach place, but is today a destination for numerous visitors of pilgrimage tourism, particularly from Myanmar, and increasingly from Thailand too since the official opening of the border in Myawaddy in 2014. Those who might think that the demanding, strenuous climb would discourage large numbers of tourists from taking on the ascent are in for a shock.

The upper platform may only be entered barefoot – and the soles of your feet will very quickly seek out the shaded areas of the sun-heated floor almost on their own. But the view is worth all the effort: further peaks of the massif are crowned by smaller ritual structures; below are the vast plains of the Thanlwin, used agriculturally and densely populated; other limestone summits rise up in the background.

Address 97°40'7.12" E 16°49'27.05" N | **Getting there** From Thaton on the NH85 around 26 miles to the bridge over the Thanlwin, turn right after 1.2 more miles, left after another 1.2 miles, then after 2.5 miles enter Lumbini Buddha Garden and climb to Zwegabin; from Mawlamyine about 35 miles; from Hpa-an around 7 miles and a shorter, very sporty direct climb possible from the east side | **Tip** You can watch the fishermen throwing out their cast nets on the many lakes around the mountain.

61 Kyauk Ka Lat Pagoda
In the middle of the primordial ocean

The view is breathtaking: blue lakes, lush green rice paddies, rugged mountain chains, steeply towering needles of rock all around. At the end of the rainy season the landscape is immersed in the most intense colours. From the peak of the rock, which you can climb to the small monastery, you look out onto the spectacular karst landscape of the region around Hpa-an. Countless caves and grottos with impressive stalactite formations are hidden in the parallel forested mountain chains and the individual, steep tower and cone karst rocks. In many caves there is evidence of prehistoric settlers. Today there are stupas, shrines and altars here. More and more caves are developed and opened up for visits.

The deeper meaning in climbing to the top of the rock for the locals lies not, of course, in enjoying the beautiful view, but rather in visiting the monastery. However, the two are not in conflict: to delight in beauty and to be inspired to wonder and look, is part of the meditative experience of being outside the mundane. You climb, in the truest sense, into higher spheres. This is based on notions from Indian cosmology, which arrived in Myanmar with Buddhism: a tall mountain, especially one standing alone in water, symbolises the sacred Mount Meru. Around this seat of the gods, to which all spheres of the world are oriented, is the primordial ocean, circular and divided into individual spheres by ring walls. The inhabited Earth is divided into the four quarters of heaven by two axes and limited in its extent by the primordial ocean.

In the real world they are natural or artificially installed mountains and bodies of water with monasteries placed on top. The hierarchically tiered central-peripheral spheres of existence are architecturally staggered in large temple complexes. The four terraces of decreasing height, oriented to the compass points, lie concentrically around the symbolic centre of the world.

Address 97°38'25.98" E 16°49'6.36" N | Getting there 2.5 miles west of Lumbini Buddha Garden | Hours All day | Tip Around 7 miles from the centre of Hpa-an on the AH1 towards the southeast, next to the Kaw Ka Thaung Cave, is a swimming pool fed by a spring, ready to provide refreshment.

62 __ Saddan Cave
Great darkness with bats

On the southern end of the mountain range that culminates in Zwe-gabin, the water has created a long cave in the limestone massif. It is only one of several caves near Hpa-an that are accessible to visitors. For the Buddhist population it is both an excursion destination and a place of worship, for foreign visitors a remote attraction. Respect for religious practices demands that outsiders also only enter the cave barefoot.

A huge hall opens up behind the rather unassuming entrance, sub-divided by small ground sills or limestone concretions with individual stalagmites and stalactites. The path for the visitor snakes around one mile through the cave system, steps overcome the difference in height between individual sections, which seem like sequential chambers and give rise to ever new views, even in the scant lighting.

Not all sections of the cave are natural. In the front part espe-cially, the walls are partly stabilised with concrete, a practise that is found in numerous caves in Southeast Asia. Some side caves are closed off so that visitors don't get lost. You come across religious and mythological figures time and again on the tour through the cave: a large lying Buddha, countless small golden Buddha figures and animal shapes integrated into the rock. Once you reach the main exit, your view is directed towards the tropical landscape. From here the way back to the car park is possible either by boat or on foot via a narrow path.

The drive to the cave is in itself fascinating; the site is approached on unpaved roads, which lead through rural settlements with simple dwellings that are still covered with dried leaves in the traditional manner, and through expanses of farmland with rice paddies. One can often watch fishermen on the edges of rice paddies throwing out their nets and taking the catch back into the villages in wicker bas-kets by bike or motorbike.

Address 97°43'7.42" E 16°44'23.72" N | Getting there Around 7 miles from Lumbini Buddha Garden, west along the mountain ridge on unpaved local roads to the car park at Saddan Cave | Tip There's a rich abundance of bird life to be found nesting in holes in the steep karst rocks of the area.

63 __ Commuters

The open border to Thailand

The crossing of the last mountain ridge on the way from Hpa-an to Myawaddy has drivers in awe: the AH1, part of the Asian Highway Network, winding and sometimes steep because of the differences in height, was beaten through the mountain range with enormous, artificially terraced embankments, a Myanmar-Thailand joint effort that is evidence of the growing economic influence of the neighbouring country to the east. Thanks to this route, it is no longer necessary to use the original road over the mountains, where the direction of travel alternates on a daily basis. A lively city has grown directly on the border, in which Thai car and motorbike number plates appear. Beyond passport inspection, the modern friendship bridge spans the border river Thaungyin/Moei; a lane change takes place in the middle, as Myanmar introduced right-hand traffic after separating from the British Empire, while they drive on the left in Thailand.

A few yards further on, the border can be crossed in another way: motorboats for 10 to 20 people cover the short distance from the steps of the landing area on the Myanmar side to the natural bank on the Thai border within about a minute. Once you become aware of the situation you will also discover small groups of people walking to the landing point on the riverbank on the Thai side. These are mainly daily commuters from Myanmar, looking for work on the Thai side. Investors from Thailand, China, Japan, Korea and other Asian countries have located numerous companies in labour-intensive textile industries here in Mae Sot.

This informal border crossing cannot be recommended to foreigners, as the return would be an illegal entry, and the entry stamp needed upon leaving Thailand would be missing. But the border has been open to foreigners since August 2014; they can pass through the regular processing on the bridgeheads.

Address 98°30'59.17" E 16°41'27.86" N, Myawaddy | Getting there Take AH1 to the
Thaungyin/Moei border river | Tip At the west entrance to Myawaddy, around 100 yards
east of the City Petroleum Thai Cuisine Restaurant, on both sides of the Myawaddy-Thin
Gan Nyi Naung Road, is the interesting transhipment centre of Thai-Myanmar trade.

64___Railway Memorial
The unknown end of Death Railway

Do you remember the book and the film *The Bridge on the River Kwai?* The western terminus of the over 250-miles-long railway route that the Japanese occupiers built between Thailand and Burma during World War II, is now marked 40 miles south of Mawlamyine by a short section of rail and the restored locomotive engine C5031. The three concrete figures in front represent a Japanese soldier and two prisoners of war. The museum provides information with maps and photos.

The railway was built in haste by prisoners of war and forced labour – the estimate is 55,000 prisoners of war and more than 200,000 forced labourers. The hard working conditions (long hours, little food, disease, inadequate tools and harsh punishment for the smallest of transgressions) cost the lives of thousands of people. There are no exact figures; estimates range from 16,000 to 82,000 people. The rail route was completed on 17 October, 1943. However, the railway was only in operation for 17 months, even though it created a connection to the Burmese coastal railway.

Close by, inaugurated by General Aung San in 1946, is the second-biggest war cemetery in Myanmar with 3,771 graves. The memorial is to the Allied soldiers who lost their lives in the battle against the Japanese or during the building of the 'Death Railway'. The Commonwealth War Graves Commission supervises the complex.

The south of Myanmar is still relatively unknown to tourists. Today's Kyaikkami, 15 miles northwest of Thanbyuzayat, was known as Amherst in the British colonial era, a place from which missionaries went out into Southeast Asia and which served the British as a bathing town. To this day you can view evidence of the active congregational life during the British period in the town's Christian churches, in the form of donations and commemorative plaques or craftwork.

Address 97°43'46.04" E 15°57'23.24" N, Thanbyuzayat | Getting there From Mawlamyne around 40 miles southwards to Thanbyuzayat, museum site around 1 mile south of the city centre, on the left side after crossing the railway tracks | Hours Death Railway Museum and park: daily 10am–4pm, admission fee applicable | Tip It is worth visiting the memorial at the World War II cemetery on the main road west of the rail crossing.

65   Pagoda in the Sea
Wade or wait

At high tide there is no escape, you just have to wait until the tide goes out again to get back to the mainland on foot. As the surf is violent and the waves unpredictable, boats can't moor here either. In short, it's a place for temporary solitude, contemplation and intro-spection. A rock sticking up out of the sludge of low tide probably inspired the idea to build a small stupa in the sea. It is certainly very picturesque, defying the force of the waves at high tide, embedded in the all-embracing sea.

The stupa is part of the Kyaikkhami Yele Pagoda, which was built on a flat rock on the edge of the sea and is said to house several strands of Buddha's hair. The solid ground facilitated the early settle-ment by the sea. Kyaikkhami has 'changed ownership' several times in the course of its eventful history. The town – called Chiang Kran at the time – temporarily belonged to the large Thai Ayutthaya King-dom, which was destroyed in 1767. The British renamed it Amherst in the course of the First Anglo-Burmese War (1824–1826), after the city (as well as the two coastal regions of Arakan and Tenas-serim, today's Rakhine State and Tanintharyi Region) was seized under William Amherst, 1st Earl Amherst, who would later become Governor-General of India. Afterwards they created a kind of first capital here, with the establishment of their military headquarters, even though the city was never officially given this status. The cultural heritage of British rule is still very much present.

The oldest church in Myanmar commemorates the American mis-sionary Adoniram Judson (1788–1850), the first to work for many years in the country. Together with his wife, Ann, he not only com-piled the first translation of the Bible into Burmese, but also created the first Burmese-English dictionary; they also translated a catechism and several books into Burmese. Adoniram was buried at sea, while Ann's grave can be visited in Kyaikkhami.

Address 97°33'28.14" E 16°4'56.90" N, Kyaikkhami | Getting there On the NH8, 40 miles from Mawlamyine south to Thanbyuzayat, then turn right towards Kyaikkhami, following the road 15 miles to the end. Walk through the covered corridor to the pagoda; at low tide take the narrow path on the north corner to the small pagoda on the rocks | Tip It's worth taking a detour to the locally very popular Setse Beach on the Gulf of Martaban between Thanbyuzayat and Kyaikkami. It's a very lively beach, but you shouldn't expect white sand!

66 Fishermen's Quarter

Freshly dried fish

The smell is overwhelming, and living here very hard to imagine. The source is quickly identified: fish or octopus drying on wooden frames or grids, or shrimp laid out on tarpaulins to dry. The wooden houses near the harbour stand on stilts in the flood-prone area, with basic sanitary facilities in tiny gardens, drinking water supplied by tanker lorries – and with major sewage problems.

Not until around 550 yards away from the shore do the buildings change to permanent houses. But here too there are drying frames and women busy gutting the fresh fish and cutting them either into long strips or skilfully fanning them out in star shapes for the drying process. It's not uncommon to also see shark fins, a delicacy for the Chinese market – or small whale sharks. It is illegal to fish and sell the latter, but it often ends up on the fish market as bycatch. Despite the acrid smell, it is exciting to observe how the fish is processed, from landing to sale and then to its preparation and drying.

All of this is to be found in Fishermen's Quarter, near the harbour of the biggest city in Tanintharyi in south Myanmar. Myeik, or Mergui as it was called during the colonial era, is the biggest fish landing centre on the region's more than 750 miles of coastline – not including the coasts of its more than 800 islands. Fishing is predominant in the traditional economy. There is small-scale, primarily subsistence fishing, and then commercially run trawlers, for export to Yangon and especially to Thailand. Myeik is not only the biggest dried fish area, but also famous throughout the country for its fish or shrimp paste: Ngapi, the hot and salty paste made of finely chopped fermented fish, has pride of place on every lunch table.

Myeik's complex history is still documented today by numerous historical buildings. Admire pagodas, churches, mosques, public and private colonial buildings on a heritage walk through the city centre.

Address 98°36'2.41" E 12°25'44.16" N, Fishermen's Quarter, Myeik | Getting there West of the airfield between two canals and the harbour, southeast of the city centre | Tip It's exciting to go on a guided day tour to special workshops and small industrial plants (broom factory, cashew nut processing factory, spring roll paper factory, lobster storage, soft-shell crab farm, etc.). Make sure to savour snack time in the tea shops, popular among locals.

67 __ Village on the Coast
Destruction and reconstruction

An embankment on a coast – who's never come across such a thing built in order to protect the people from the sea? From the daily tide, from the springtide and storm surges – from tsunamis and tropical cyclones too? In Mingalar Thaungthan you get an idea of how differently humans can react to a catastrophe.

After a journey lasting many hours in a narrow motorboat from Pathein through the Ayeyarwady Delta towards the coast, through the countless tributaries and creeks of the river, you reach waterways lined by nipa palms, becoming ever narrower – that's why the boat has to be narrow too. The mangrove forests become ever thicker, you see the many respiratory roots of the mangroves growing upwards, mudskippers sliding through the sludge, billions of small fish and snails. Back on land you are still a half-hour walk away from the village on the coast.

In the middle of the endless flat expanse of the delta you suddenly spot an embankment a good 65 feet tall, one mile long und 50 feet wide – a piled-up wall of earth, on top of it a gravel road. Behind it, the village. Behind that? Attempts at an explanation remain lacking: To protect the village and road from the backwater of the masses of water flowing back to the sea in the monsoon? Because the people built the houses on the sea side of the embankment in order to be nearer to the boats that they put out to sea to fish? You won't find any logical answer. But you will hear about how the village was rebuilt after the devastating cyclone Nargis, which claimed almost 200,000 lives and robbed almost two and a half million people of their livelihoods in 2008. A generous private donor sponsored the reconstruction. Around 100 simple, uniform houses on short stilts give the people hope again. The embankment: it wasn't there back then. But would it even have helped against Nargis? The waves were up to 20 feet tall in places.

Address 95°48'27.75" E 16°10'0.76" N, Mingalar Thaungthan | **Getting there** From Pyapon a 2-hour motorboat journey south on the Pyapon River, after around 8.5 nautical miles (9.8 miles) east into the Kyon tut gyi Chaung, the winding canal, to Kyon Lut Ta Man (4.8 nautical miles, 5.5 miles), on foot through rice paddies, past shrimp pools around 2 miles to Mingalar Thaungthan | **Hours** Ask for a boat transfer into the delta at your hotel or the market in Pyapon | **Tip** Depending on the water level, you can sail in the ever narrower and shallower canals to Mya Sein Kann. A walk to Kyon Lut Ta Man makes sense for the way back, along the nipa palm-lined canals. Look out the remaining debris from the 2008 cyclone.

68 __ Colonial Quarter
A complex past

With your first sight of Pathein you will see almost everything that makes the city what it is: the widely visible pagoda and the busy riverbank. The city is old and was important – especially in the times when global routes predominantly went over the sea. This is the way that Buddhism reached Myanmar under Emperor Ashoka (304–232 BC) and according to legend, the Shwemokhtaw Pagoda was also established in this period.

Then everything changed fundamentally with the European colonial era. But for Pathein it would be too simple to reduce the epoch to 'the British' or to talk of 'the colonial era' as one phase, and it didn't begin in 1824 with the First Anglo-Burmese War. In fact, the Portuguese were the first Europeans to colonise, when they expanded their system of '*carreiras*', or roadways, into mainland Southeast Asia back in 1511, after the capture of Malacca. Their trading network stretched all the way to Cosmin, as Pathein was called at the time. The Portuguese also supported the kings of Arakan and Burma with defence technology and logistics. After 1610 they were displaced by the Dutch, especially the powerful Dutch East India Company, who themselves lost influence after 1795 in the course of the later expansion of the British East India Trading Company. After winning the war in 1826, the British developed Pathein, with a fortress and harbour, into a garrison and trading place for the export of raw materials from the interior.

Those who set off on a tour of discovery will sense the eventful story of the city's genesis: stately colonial buildings in very original condition stand in the busy main roads of the centre, as well as on the large estates in the residential area to the east. Real gems are the only two rice mills that are still steam-powered: the Sein Myitta Nal Myay Rice Mill still uses the machinery the British imported from Ipswich.

Address 94°43'56.32" E 16°46'40.27" N, Merchant Street/corner of Bwat Kyi Tan Road, Pathein | Getting there South of the central market and Shwe Pyi Thar market | Tip It is also worth taking the ferry across to the west bank from where you have a wonderful view of the former colonial city.

69__ Umbrella Makers' Quarter

Family handicraft with global fame

155 miles before reaching the ocean, Myanmar's longest river, the Ayeyarwady, starts to spread out into a huge delta area that grows to over 95 miles wide. The colonial harbour city Pathein, located on one of the big western outflows, the Pathein or Nga-Wun River at the foot of the southern foothills of the Rakhine Mountains, is the capital of this region. It is not only one of the most important transhipment points for rice, but also an important crafts centre of globally famous umbrella makers.

The colourful decorative umbrellas are produced in family-run businesses in sizes from 11 inches to over 120 inches in diameter in a finely tuned collaborative process. The basic framework – made out of thin bamboo rods, threaded into a bamboo hub, attached to a lathed bamboo stick – is covered with cotton fabric and artfully decorated with black ornaments on various coloured backgrounds. Easy to open and close with a laced closing mechanism and waterproofed with a coat of special varnish, they serve as parasols at wedding receptions, as decorative objects in spacious households and, in the plainer red-brown version, as protection from the sun for monks.

One of the old family businesses which is famous even beyond Myanmar is the Shwe Sar Umbrella Workshop. Behind the offices, the employees sit in the workshop on slightly elevated bamboo platforms, surrounded by bamboo rods, pots of glue and paint, strings and cotton fabric, lit by individual rays of sun that shine through narrow cracks in the ceiling, fabricating the wonderful umbrellas, step by step, in perfect harmony. The colourful collection of umbrellas, mainly in red, orange, yellow, green and blue, composed of all the different sizes, drying on the lawn of the backyard and glowing in the sun, is a very special sight.

Address 94°44'45.77" E 16°47'32.44" N, Min Yat Tan Road, Pathein | Getting there From the harbour, 1.2 miles east via Kozu Road, Tadargyidan Road and Pathein Road, then turn left onto Sakawar Road, after 440 yards turn right into Min Yat Tan Road to Shwe Sar Umbrella Workshop | Tip Equally worth seeing are the small shipyards along Kanna Road in the southwest of the city and also on the opposite bank.

70__Fishermen's Village
Cooked or dried

Why do all Myanmar tour operators send foreign tourists to the dream beaches in Ngwe Hsaung and Ngapali? Is it just because the sand is not as white in Chaungtha or is there a fear that the standard is just not high enough? Neither of these should stop a Myanmar enthusiast from taking a trip to the most lively beach on the west coast of the Ayeyarwady Region, especially frequented by locals from the Yangon Region as it is quick to reach for short trips.

Alongside the colourful hustle and bustle on the bathing beach you also have the chance to discover traditional coastal fishing. In order to escape the excitement of the fun-seeking and relaxation-thirsty, you simply follow the water line to the south and after a swing to the east you'll find yourself in a completely different world. Simple bamboo and wood huts under palm trees, firm silty sand at low tide, mangroves evidently cleared for open access to the water, small- and medium-sized fishing boats and large bamboo platforms for the drying of fish point towards a typical fishing and snail-collecting settlement.

Apart from a couple of children and some people on the platforms, which are up to two metres high, sorting fish heads, fillets and offal for drying, there is hardly anyone here. The men and often the older children too are fishing or collecting mussels and snails. On the platforms or in the private houses the women process the caught and collected animals: once topped and gutted, the fish are laid out in strips to dry. Molluscs such as the spider conch, the chiton, trochus snails or diverse genera of the nerites family are cooked or dried and the shells are cleaned and prepared as individual pieces or in chains for sale as welcome souvenirs for friends and family. Fresh fish, shrimp of all sizes and live crabs are offered at the market and to the multitude of restaurants, or sold to the snack-sellers on the beach.

Address 94°26'22.62" E 16°57'10.89" N, Chaungtha | **Getting there** From Pathein around 40 miles via Rakhine Yoma to Chaungtha, Chaungtha Road to the beach, on the beach turn left | **Tip** You can get to the new beach north of Chaungtha by motorbike taxi – a roughly 4-mile trip through coconut groves and along the beach.

71 Aung Mingalar Island

Petrified under your feet

Tourists often associate a holiday in Southeast Asia with sun, sand and sea. In Myanmar it is areas near Ngwe Hsaung, Ngapali and Chaungtha on the west coast that attract local and foreign holiday-makers with their elongated beaches and a multitude of bays and upstream islands. The journey there is not really the destination, as it is an arduous trip through the Rakhine Mountains, spurs of the over 750-mile-long Indo-Burma Range, that stretch from the Himalayas to the Andaman Sea and form the western geological unit of Myanmar. In the southern course, the range presents itself as sparsely populated, covered with secondary forest and tree plantations, tightly staggered chains of hills with a maximum height of 410 feet that reach down to the narrow coastal landscape. The sight of sandy-yellow to white, fine sand beaches, black rocks with bizarre erosion patterns, palm trees and blue sea is therefore all the more pleasing.

Only few are aware that here they find themselves in the geological collision zone of the Indian and south Eurasian continental plates, where unimaginable powers caused the pushing together and slanting of massive rock formations and contributed to the creation of the Rakhine Mountains. Clear evidence of these processes, which began over 50 million years ago, are the shift sequences of the Indo-Burma flysch, prominent in the intertidal zone that even a geological novice can make out. These are dark grey to black sand, silt and clay stone deposits that slipped down the underwater continental slope in the course of orogeny (mountain formation), stratified and later lifted to slanting or vertical with increasing pressure. These striking, ripple-like, 2- to 8-inch-thick sediment layers appear as 'stone waves' especially in the western areas of the upstream islands. Aung Mingalar/Phoe Kalar Island is one of the places where very ancient geological formations can be discovered in secluded bays on a relaxing island tour.

Address 94°25'30.07" E 16°56'53.52" N | Getting there From beach section at the end of Chaungtha Road with the boat to Aung Mingalar Island (also Chaungtha Kyun), circle the island anticlockwise, formations of 'stone waves' on the whole west and south sides of the island | Hours Boat transit 200 kyat per person | Tip In the tea shops on the north side of the island you can enjoy cold drinks with your feet in the sea and a view of the colourful activity on Chaungtha Beach.

72— Coastal Swamp Rice Farms
Wet feet for lunch

A white sandy beach bordered by blue sea under green palm fronds – a poetic description of the colours here could go on and on. Travellers associate tropical coasts with images of desire and relaxation. But not everyone sees it that way. If you suppress the romantic associations for a moment, beach and coast are in fact very bleak habitats: dangerous because of the wild influences of sea and storms, unsafe because of the dangers of external invaders, infertile because of sandy and saline soils. The natural vegetation doesn't provide much help either: mangroves, palms, casuarinas – you can't live well off them.

What luck that there are the coastal swamps (apart from the mosquitoes). Looking inland from the sea, you can see them in the area behind the barrier beach. Backwater from the mainland gathers here, but sometimes these are also self-contained lagoons, which initially still have water in them, but silt up little by little, because the water evaporates, the wind blows sand or soil into the hollows or plants die and earth develops. From time to time the sea reaches the swamps again, for example at springtide or during storm surges, so that the water there is brackish and more saline than further inland.

The fishermen in the few coastal villages have made a virtue of necessity – as you can't live from fish alone, they began to develop the coastal swamps for the cultivation of rice. Even if the harvests are less productive because of the poorer soils then elsewhere, they grow enough for their own self-sufficiency. Paddy rice growing is very labour-intensive: the sowing, often in planting beds, takes place in the dry season, and in the rainy season the tussocks of rice have to be replanted. The harvest follows after the end of the rainy season. Still, it is convenient that the rice harvest finishes around the time the tourism season begins.

Address 94°23'21.83" E 16°51'33.46" N | Getting there Coming from Pathein, turn left to the northwest before the barrier beach | Tip A visit to the elephant camp on the way to Ngwe Hsaung, around 23 miles west of Pathein or 10 miles east of Ngwe Hsaung in the Rakhine Mountains (clear signpost on the road), is highly recommended.

73__Silver Beach
The ultimate beach

Christmas or New Year under palm trees on a beach? That might not be to everyone's taste, and if you do decide it's for you, there's the threat of encountering crowds in the places with the supposedly most beautiful tropical sunsets. Unlike Ngapali further north, Ngwe Hsaung offers a pleasant mixture of conviviality and peace to those who are looking for a little less action. The (Western) turn of the year is a cool season for the lowlands of Myanmar, in which you may wish to refuel on the sun's heat. Along the coast of the Bay of Bengal the resorts line up one after the other.

The view from outside will give you a sense of the differences in price and prestige. In the less-expensive resorts the power genera-tors do not run continuously 24 hours a day, but observe a reasonable night-time curfew, and not all of the bungalows are equipped with air conditioning, whereas in the higher-priced resorts every room is air conditioned. There, the restaurants may also offer a larger selection of food, but when you sit outside on a plain terrace almost on top of the water in the evening as the sun is setting, you'll get that hol-iday feeling no matter what. If you take a walk on the beach that is accessible to everyone, at some resorts you'll still be able to make out the consequences of Nargis, the catastrophic cyclone in April/May 2008. Others, however, exhibit their absolute will to rebuild and redevelop.

Those who want to experience the days around the turn of the year in not quite such a lazy way can take a motorbike taxi and be driven over several miles of sand beach – perhaps to the water sports resort of the 2013 Asian Games, or to the fishing boats of the village. And even a walk through the village is appealing, simply because the plethora of souvenirs that are sold almost everywhere you go is not on offer here, and because the shops on the main road are more like a large market.

Address 94°23'36.88" E 16°46'41.21" N | Getting there South from Ngwe Hsaung village on the beach, past Lovers Island around 6 miles to the mouth of a small river | Tip A bike trip along the beach to Sinma Beach is a lovely experience that can be combined well with a visit to the village of Sinma.

74___Access to the World's Oceans

Development would be most welcome

The Burmese word *sittwe* means 'place where the war meets'. Here in 1784 the troops of the Burmese King Bodawpaya crushed the much smaller army of the Arakan kingdom. Afterwards they captured their capital of Mrauk U and assimilated the region of Arakan (today: Rakhine State) into the Burmese kingdom. Many ethnic Rakhine have not forgotten this occupation to this day and press for their own rights and identity. After the First Anglo-Burmese War, in 1826, the British relocated the regional capital from Mrauk-U to Sittwe (then Akyab) and developed the city into a sea harbour. In this way Sittwe, like many other coastal cities, grew in the course of colonial-era seafaring and the trade in raw materials, from a small fishing village into an important harbour, which was mainly used to export rice, and military base.

Most travellers only come for a stopover in Sittwe on their way to see the old royal city of Mrauk-U. But those who wish to understand a bit more about the historic contexts of the region and its chances in the future should spend a bit of time on an exploration of Sittwe and in encountering its people. On the newly designed promenade, 'The Point', where the Kaladan River flows into the Indian Ocean, you will grasp the enormous strategic importance of the city and port location. You can see the effects of the colonial era in many old buildings, including two churches, and in the fact that a high proportion of the population of migrants originate from today's India and Bangladesh. The recent outbreaks of the long-standing conflicts multiplies the tragic burden of the region, for which there are no simple solutions. A planned deep-sea harbour project nearby compounds the situation. Comprehensive development for all, from supplies and peace to education and work, is urgently needed.

Address 92°54'11.09" E 20°8'28.96" N, Kanner Street, Sittwe | Getting there Harbour facility at the central market, access to pier through the central market street | Tip You can walk or take a trishaw taxi 2 miles south on the promenade (Shu Khin Tha Street) to the popular destination with viewing tower and beach.

75__ The Mahamuni Museum
Loss of the most sacred

The famous Mahamuni Buddha of Mandalay is, alongside the Shwedagon Pagoda, one of Myanmar's most highly venerated shrines. But it wasn't here from the beginning – it was in fact removed from elsewhere. More than 200 years ago, when King Bodawpaya sent out his oldest son to conquer the kingdom of Rakhine in 1784, he had the Mahamuni image brought to his capital of Amarapura. The statue was moved from here after the relocation of the capital to Mandalay.

The name Mahamuni is from the Pali and means 'The Great Sage'. In order to grasp the eminent significance of this Mahamuni Buddha, you need to understand the history of its creation, which is described in chronicles such as the manuscript 'Sappadana pakarana'.

According to legend, Gautama Buddha visited the first capital of Arakan, Dhanyawaddy, around 190 miles northeast of Sittwe, 554 years before Christ, on his missionary journey to spread Buddhism. The king of Arakan and thousands of followers paid homage to the Buddha and asked him to allow a true to life effigy of him to be made – there are only five of its kind. The effigy was created in seven days in Buddha's presence, and he himself enlivened and consecrated it. The original shrine of the image, in which it stood for 2,338 years, was in the Kyauktaw Pagoda. In a small museum, numerous remarkable finds from the time of its construction are exhibited, including heads, busts and stone tablets of the Buddha.

Even though the source studies question whether Gautama Buddha had ever personally entered the area of today's Myanmar and suggest that the likeness was first created in the 4th century AD, it is still the oldest in Myanmar by a long way. In the Pyu cities of Beikthano and Halin, established shortly after the turn of the first millennium, there are no Buddha statues. You will find them in Sri Ksetra, but the statues there are dated between the 7th and 9th centuries.

Address 93°3'47.71" E 20°52'15.99" N | Getting there Kyauktaw Mahamuni Buddha Image, around 7 miles east of Kyauktaw on the road to Mrauk-U | Hours All day | Tip Get an impressive view over the Kaladan River to the city of Kyauktaw from the Kyauktaw Mountain Pagoda. The staircase is right next to the bridge over the Kaladan on the east bank.

76___Pyay Night Market
Light, air and fried food

Although Pyay, with its over 130,000 inhabitants, is the second-biggest city on the Ayeyarwady after Mandalay, it seems very sedate. Most travellers see the old trading city as more of a through station on the north-south Yangon-Bagan Highway or on the east-west route to the beach in Ngapali or into Rakhine State. This situation has improved a little since the old Pyu city, Sri Ksetra, was named a World Heritage Site by UNESCO in 2015. Ever since, tourist ships have brought numerous visitors to the city's small harbour. Today you will occasionally encounter river cruise ships. For tourists who wish to travel a little off the beaten track of the classic, often over-filled attractions, Pyay is a good place to explore the city life of a main regional city in a relaxed way. The position on the river, the colonial remnants, the buildings from various religions and lots of restaurants with typical regional cuisine characterise the image of the city. Among the important sights are the central Shwe Sandaw Pagoda east of the big roundabout and the neighbouring, 10-storey, sitting Buddha (Sehtatgyi Pagoda).

A little less imposing but no less interesting, the night market is just west of the roundabout, on the Old Post Office Road that leads to the river. It is not the light of streetlamps that illuminates the market as darkness falls, but rather the brightly shining neon strips of the mobile stalls and street kitchens that flood the space in front with light. All you can see above is the pitch black of the night sky. An airy breeze from the river carries the smell of fried food and various curry and vegetable dishes through the market, and it really isn't easy to decide what to have for dinner. On many stalls, local snacks made from the beans and other pulses grown in this region as well as peanuts and sesame, often combined with honey, are on offer – the ideal take-away dessert for the evening walk along the river, for locals and tourists alike.

Address 95°12'54.15" E 18°49'12.15" N, Old Post Office Road, Pyay | **Getting there** From
the roundabout on the NH2/Main Road at Pyay Main Station straight to the Ayeyarwady
River | **Tip** A motorbike tour to the Shwe Bon Thar Muni and Phoe Oo Taung pagodas
located on mountain ridges on the west bank of the Ayeyarwady opens up wide views of the
agricultural landscape around Pyay and the narrow valley of the Ayeyarwady to the north
(over Nawaday bridge, around 15 miles).

77___Baw Baw Gyi Pagoda
Standing in a rice field

Around five miles from today's Pyay is the deserted ancient city of Sri Ksetra (pronounced 'Thiri Kittiya' in Myanmar). Southeast of its city walls is an old, almost 127-feet-tall, architecturally plain stupa in the middle of open landscape, the Baw Baw Gyi Pagoda – the oldest pagoda in Myanmar. It was built in the 5th century under King Duttabaung; old chronicles mention that relics of Buddha were kept in it. The cylinder-shaped stupa with a flat cone standing on a tiered, round platform is built of brick. Around two-thirds of it is hollow.

Sri Ksetra had – as can be discerned to this day in the remains of the ramparts – an almost round floor plan. It was the last and southernmost capital of the Pyu. It was also huge. With a circumference of more than eight miles and around 3,460 acres of surface area, it was larger than Bagan or Mandalay at the peak of their respective royal powers. Only part of the city complex has been researched so far. A double protective wall with moats in the middle encircled the city, the brick ramparts were almost 16 feet tall, and 12 gates linked it with the outside world. Apparently, settlements were only found in the southern half of the city with a palace, monasteries and houses; in the north were rice fields, so that the city could withstand long sieges.

The Pyu realm of city-states existed between 200 BC and around 900 AD, long before the arrival of the Burmese in the central area of today's Myanmar. Sri Ksetra, founded in the 5th or 6th century, became the capital of Pyu in the 7th or 8th century, until the Burmese took over dominion in the 9th century and ruled from the new capital, Bagan.

In 2014, the three Pyu cities of Halin, Beikthano and Sri Ksetra became the first places in Myanmar to be named World Heritage Sites by UNESCO.

Address 95°17'8.07" E 18°47'10.48" N | Getting there Sri Ksetra, southwards from the museum through the Rahanda Gate, past the burial ground, follow left road to the pagoda | Hours All day | Tip For a very good view of the old city's double wall structure with moats, head to the bridge on 2nd Street in the new district south of the airfield, 330 yards south of the triangular junction.

78__ Burial Grounds
Respect for shards

At first glance there's very little to see in Sri Ksetra – especially if you already know, with a keen interest in archaeology, the grandiose pagoda fields of Bagan. Yet upon closer inspection you will begin to grasp that there is a hitherto hardly known, significantly older part of Myanmar's history to be discovered here. Highly interesting excavations, run by the Ministry of Culture with foreign assistance, are bringing a much deeper history to light. Alongside remnants of the Pyu culture above ground there are underground treasures: fields of graves and urns. Thus far, almost 20 have been investigated, most of which are on the edge or within walking distance of the old city walls. They stand out in the form of around 130- by 65-feet mounds of earth; up to 1,000 urns were found in each of the hills studied. The analysis so far has shown that the dead were buried with great care and that they were given objects, such as pearls, knives or bells, to take with them. In the case of a cremation, the remains of bones and ashes were buried in urns. So far, scientists have been unable to carry out precise dating and no conclusions have yet been drawn about the social class of the dead.

During the excavations, the sites have to be protected against the weather, and organic materials such as bones, but also wood and plant remains are stored in cool, dry cooling houses. After making an inventory, many of the earth hills have been carefully closed up again in order to prevent water from entering and destroying the finds. Carefully researched panels provide visitors with descriptive background information on the old burial culture.

It is noteworthy that the excavations are not only systematically documented by scientists, but are also attended by anthropologists who make sure that the bones are handled with respect. Representatives of religions and inhabitants of Pyay, who are assumed to be descendants of the dead, are also involved.

Address 95°16'43.17" E 18°47'15.54" N | Getting there Sri Ksetra, southwards from the museum through the Rahanda Gate to the burial grounds | Tip A visit to Sri Ksetra Museum in the centre of the World Heritage Site with its very informative exhibition of excavation finds is worthwhile and is also an ideal starting point to explore the central palace grounds.

79_ Graben Meander
Seen from the air, discovered on the ground

If you look out the window of an airplane on a flight from east to west (or the other way around) at a latitude of 23 degrees north, between Mingin and Falam or Hakha and suddenly become aware of a strange phenomenon – a broad, light, flat strip in the middle of dark green forests and mountains – then you have discovered it: the graben that the Taungdwin River traverses. (A graben is the depressed block of the Earth's crust that lies between two parallel faults.) It is rare to see such a phenomenon so clearly.

The scenery is also fascinating on a satellite image: you can make out the innumerable bends in the river in all their detail and the villages on the banks with the countless small, human-made terraces for rice cultivation. And even in the winding river bed you can make out how freely the water channels its path, how ramified the whole network of its flow is. In some places you discover cut-off meanders, that mark old river courses, tributaries from small side valleys, silted-up bank areas – and the course of the Monywa-Kalay Highway, safe from the high water up on the slope.

When you drive through the valley, more details come to light: ruggedly bordered by steep mountain flanks, the river winds through the up-to-two-mile-wide 'valley'. It is as if sharp borders had been drawn with a ruler: it can flow this far east or west and no further. The road on the upper slope enables an outstanding overview of the situation: above the largely closed forests, which are hardly used but seem to stand quite sparsely, you sometimes see vertical ridges tiered one after another. They are almost impossible to cross, apart from in the side valleys. Below, you see neat villages, mostly with around 100 inhabitants, connected by a few paths, fields with rice and vegetables, maize and pulses. Cattle graze on the harvested fields. The graben: an elongated island with diverse agricultural uses between the forested peaks.

Address 94°23'24.43" E 22°45'3.16" N | Getting there From Monywa on the Monywa-Kalewa Highway around 85 miles to the northwest between Tongyi and Kyabin | Tip A picturesque morning drive through the graben with stops in the villages is a special experience.

80 — The Dividing Kaladan
Only by barque and barge

Paletwa, a picturesque place in the southeastern periphery of Chin State, is a full day's journey away from the coastal city of Sittwe. When you leave the only two-lane country road in the region, which was surfaced just a few years ago, near Kyauktaw, you suddenly find yourself in a secluded area: loosely forested, very rural areas with occasional small villages. The gravel road crosses numerous ridges, twists along steep slopes, and on high banks you can often grab a glimpse of the Kaladan River, which meanders in a valley growing ever narrower to the north. All it takes is a powerful downpour for you to realise why a journey in a vehicle without four-wheel drive would be over in a flash: the vehicle scrabbles through deep puddles and mud; bridges are swamped. Shortly before reaching a tributary, the road turns, winding to the steep banks of the Kaladan. This is where the journey ends for all vehicles. Following a narrow footpath on foot, you finally reach a few provisional huts and an unsecured landing for small boats.

It takes a good half hour to ferry across to Paletwa, and you grasp how much the river divides two worlds from each other. Bangladesh is only around 11 miles away, and if you continue further to the north you can reach the Indian border after around 60 miles. Lately, with the financial help of the Indian government, a modern port facility is being built across from Paletwa as part of an investment, which bears the sophisticated name Kaladan Multi-Modal Transit Transport Project. A transhipment location for commodities from India is to be developed here, which is intended to connect the cut-off far east of India with the Indian Ocean. The idyllic town with its many churches and squares is still in a deep sleep, but soon a large bridge will connect it with the other side. The intention is to connect the region with the planned new network, the Economic Corridors of the Greater Mekong Subregion, which will link Kolkata with Yangon – at some point in the far-off future.

Address 92°51'19.95" E 21°18'14.11" N | Getting there From Kyauktaw along the east side of the Kaladan to just before Paletwa (around 42 miles), then switch to boat, as bridge in development | Tip Visit the Paletwa Baptist Church on the main road.

81_ Temporary Riverside Camp

Spices on the drying mat

At first glance the huts look poor: the roofs made of intertwined leaves and branches or covered with corrugated sheets of iron, the walls made up of simple mats. The shops are strung together on a side street, and behind them towards the river, plastic sheeting and mats are spread out on the floodplain gravel and pebbles. Something is laid out to dry on them. Men, women and children regularly turn the precious commodity so that it dries more quickly in the sun. After all, the dry season is nearing its end and as soon as the first pre-monsoon rains set in in April, not only do the mats disappear, but also the provisional huts, as this is when the otherwise gently flowing Samee River begins to transform into a torrential mountain river.

The provisional huts on the flood plain are only the 'summer camp' for the locals – up above on the slope stand the families' spacious stone and wood houses. This is where they actually live, especially in the rainy season, when more than ten times the amount of rain falls in the five months of monsoon than falls all year in Central Europe. Solar panels on the roofs reveal that the town suffers from a lack of electricity; for washing you use the river. Most inhabitants live off the harvests of slash-and-burn agriculture – and in the past few years also from the increasingly lucrative revenues that can be earned growing *khamoun* and *wa-oo*, the elephant foot yam (*Amorphophallus paeoniifolius*). Both agricultural products are dried on the flood plains. Middlemen, often merchants from China or Myanmarese travelling salesmen in their pay, come to the villages at the end of the dry season and purchase the dried harvest, which they process and pack and sell on. *Khamoun* is sold for a high price on the world market, and most ends up in China. The elephant foot yam they sell is used as animal feed in chicken and pig farming.

Address 93°5'48.72" E 21°17'49.82" N | Getting there From Paletwa around 31 miles on the new road east to Samee, from the city centre (market road) to the banks of the Samee River | Tip On a walk on the slope above the river you can enjoy a wonderful view of the river valley and the temporary settlement on the flood plain, while the local swimming baths on the river are tempting.

82 __ Colonial Relic
The fire is lit

A narrow, winding road winds up to Kanpetlet from the lowlands. The town is at an altitude of between around 4,265 and 5,250 feet, which bestows it cold winter nights and refreshing coolness in the hot seasons of the year. Then, the thermometer climbs well above 40 degrees Celsius in the lowlands east of the Chin Hills, and the floodplains of the Saw Chaung, at only around 1,300 feet, mutate into a fertile breeding ground for mosquitoes.

It is no surprise therefore that the British liked to escape here during the colonial era, in order to enjoy the coolness and freshness, the morning mist, the scent of the pine forests and the clear, long-distance view over the country and to hike in the mountains or to play cricket. But, unlike in other parts of the country, almost nothing is left of this: only one house is still standing, the only witness of the British past, right by the road to Kho Num Sumg Mountain. During the British period the district office of the construction ministry was here; nearby there were other administration buildings, and higher up, the centre of the British settlement. But it was too cold that far up for the local inhabitants, so they relocated the settlement further down after World War II. Carpenters dismantled the British houses and the building material was used elsewhere. A few years ago a Myanmarese investor had the old foundations levelled and built a four-star hotel with 26 bungalows on top of it.

The former district office now belongs to the national park. A housekeeping couple make sure that it is kept in good condition. There are initial thoughts about transforming it into a museum. In the meantime you can still admire the solid stone foundations, the original doors and windows as well as the rooms with high ceilings and the soot-blackened fireplaces in the house. They, at least, remain intact, and bless the residents with light and warmth on cold winter nights.

83__Kho Num Sumg
The name of the mountain

'Biggest Mountain' – this is the name the local population gave it. They're referring to the highest mountain in the Chin Hills, which stretch around 250 miles in a north-south direction and 95 miles in an east-west direction, and mark the border region between Myanmar and India. At 10,016 feet, the mountain towers over all the other peaks of this powerful range, subdivided into numerous north-south running mountain ranges. The local population belong predominantly to the Daai ethnic group, who live with around 40,000 speakers in the four townships of Kanpetlet, Matupi, Mindat and Paletwa. As so often in mountain regions in which the villages and cities are far apart from each other, different dialects developed so that even the pronunciation and spelling of place names differ from each other. Therefore 'biggest' can also be found spelt Kawnu-soum or Khonuamthung.

But that's not all: the Burmese, who form the majority of the 135 official ethnic groups in Myanmar, gave the mountain the name Nat Ma Taung, which roughly means 'evil, devilish mountain'. It's no surprise that the Chin didn't want to use the name. Further still, when the British conquered all parts of today's Myanmar after the Third Anglo-Burmese War and also took possession of the mountain regions at end of the 19th century, they gave the mountain 'their' name: Mount Victoria, in honour of Queen Victoria. Each name is simultaneously an avowal. Out of unawareness or pragmatism, the surrounding national park, founded in 1994, only bears one name: Nat Ma Taung.

From Kanpetlet you can reach the peak on an almost one-hour drive through wild forests and extensive moorland. Hundreds of species of birds live in the pine and oak forests. Many old trees are covered in epiphytes. In the dry season, tree rhododendrons blossom lavishly in vibrant red.

Address 93°54'10.66" E 21°14'0.96" N | **Getting there** From Kanpetlet around 14 miles west; from Mindat around 25 miles south on rough road; on both routes the last 3.5 miles only passable with four-wheel drive | **Tip** Take a trekking tour with a stay in the villages, preferably when the rhododendrons are in bloom (Nov to Feb).

84___Cluster of Churches

Facets of Christian missionary work

The village of Thantlang, with a population of roughly 3,000, stretches along a broad mountain ridge, at an altitude of around 4,600 feet. The best overview is to be had from the monument in the south, from which one's first impression is of the large, colourful façades of the village's numerous churches.

The Thantlang Baptist Church is one of the oldest in Chin State. There are many more Baptist churches besides, for example the Thantlang Centenary Baptist Church, the Johnson Memorial Baptist Church, the Emmanuel Chin Baptist Church and the Chin Evangelical Baptist Church. The Mara Evangelical Church is also locally represented, the members of which mostly come from the small ethnic group the Mara. You can also visit the Thantlang Believer Church, the Church on the Rock, the United Pentecostal Church and the Seventh-Day-Adventist Church in Thantlang and the Catholic Myanmar Church.

You will inevitably be asking yourself why there is such a huge diversity of different churches here, as there are in most other places in Chin State. The explanation is to be found back in the colonial era, when the British, after they had conquered the whole territory of today's state, also advanced into the mountainous regions, with their military, their administration – and missionaries. An entourage of missionaries from many different Christian faiths arrived, wanting to encourage – from the view at the time – the uncivilised local population to develop with the help of faith and to show them the right path. The predominant local conceptions of animism, of the souls in nature and creatures, were displaced and overlaid by Christian thinking, even if many original customs have still been preserved and mixed in with religious beliefs. Today the Christian faith unites the communities and strengthens a supra-regional Chin identity beyond all linguistic and ethnic diversity, and connects them with the world.

Address 93°25'40.08" E 22°41'54.35" N | **Getting there** From the south, from Rezua via a road through beautiful landscape off the main route (Rezua-Hakha) via Hnaring (around 95 miles, day trip); can be reached from Hakha on a well-developed road in almost 3 hours | **Tip** The Hauka Bung Resort in the south of the city – reached on a narrow road past the telecommunication tower – is a local health resort, run by the Chin Disabled Organization. There are snacks and a wonderful view with a picnic area.

85__ The Hakha Landslide

When the mountain comes to town with a roar

'On 31 July, 2015', as an eyewitness reported, 'at around 11am, the middle part of the slope above the city began to move, it slid into the lake and cleaved a way further down through a gorge into the valley. The ground, made viscous and fluid like thick soup by the mass of water, flowed through the whole night and into the following afternoon. The noise and the sounds in the night were apocalyptic: you could hear the shattering and cracking of big trees and thick branches everywhere, but you couldn't see anything in the absolutely black of night. There was no light and no electricity. We really feared for our lives and our houses.' His house was a good 200 yards away from Revolutionary Lake, a lake created by the British to secure drinking water for the military and missionary town.

What had happened? A powerful tropical cyclone had dropped more than three times the normal amount of monsoon rain at the end of July. The steep edge of the slope above the lake had been partly deforested over the previous 20 years, so that the waterlogged slope slipped downwards. The landslide destroyed the houses of 1,242 families and the livelihoods of 5,232 residents. Fortunately, amazingly, no one was killed. Countless donations – rice, cooking oil, clothes, medication – mainly from other regions of Myanmar, but also from abroad, helped those affected to survive the following months. Those evacuated had to spend half a year in emergency accommodation, in gyms and in churches, before more than 400 new wooden houses could be built in another place, classed as safe, in the next dry season – by the government and with the financial support of numerous foreign aid organisations.

At least they have a roof over their heads again, but not the security and reassurance that there won't be more landslides in the future. Since many Chin have emigrated, there is a worldwide network that provides aid to their hometown.

Address 93°37'6.05" E 22°38'30.43" N | Getting there On the northwest flank of Mount Rung between the summit region and the Hakha stadium | Tip Walk the path to the Hakha Khuahlun Baptist Church that was destroyed by the landslide, around one mile downhill from the stadium, as well as to the newly built swimming baths and to huts with banana and sugarcane wine tasting.

86 Missionary Shrine
Commemorating the end of an era

After the painstaking and costly conquering and pacification of the Chin Hills, the British colonial powers enacted the Chin Hills Regulation in 1896, which paved the way for the Christianisation of the mountain areas. The missionaries Reverend Arthur Carson and his wife, Laura, from the American Baptist Mission were the first to reach Hakha, which was still a small village back then, on 15 March, 1899. In the following period they initially established a mission school, then an infirmary and charitable institutions: an orphanage and a nursing station for the poor, old and infirm. Together with the colonial facilities for the military and administration, a little city emerged.

Reverend Carson established the basis of the first Hakha Chin-English dictionary, which was completed by his wife 10 years after his death (in 1908). Laura remained as a missionary in Hakha until her retirement in 1920. A lovingly designed, pointed gabled house protects the final resting place of several missionaries as well as the first pastor from among the local Chin.

The conquering by the British changed everything for the Chin: life and economy, religion and beliefs. Before 1896, the mountains of today's Chin State had remained absolutely independent, never taken by other rulers, influenced by none of the big world religions. The population had hardly any contact with the kingdoms in the lowlands, except for short forays and military campaigns in both directions or in connection with limited trade. The inhabitants of the individual villages lived far away from one another and survived by subsistence farming in the form of slash-and-burn agriculture, growing millet and maize, and hunting and gathering in the surrounding forests. The clans often went to war against each other, where it was less to do with raw materials and land, more with the control over harvests and subjects.

Address 93°36'47.85" E 22°38'50.66" N, Lungbiak Inn Road, Hakha | Getting there 50 yards north of the Hakha Baptist Church, near Carson Hall | Hours Only upon request in the Hakha Baptist Church | Tip Visit the missionary museum with exhibits from the missionary period.

87__ Old Chin House

Prototype for the future?

Amongst traditional houses built of wood and standing on stilts and some modern stone-built family homes in a district south of Rung Mountain, an unusual house is to be found: a 2003 replica based on original plans of the house of a village chief.

The front side facing the street has a decorative wooden façade, featuring painted engravings of two hornbills – the heraldic bird of Chin State, a warrior with costume and weapons, the skulls of forest buffalo (*gayal* or *mithun*) and typical geometric Chin garland patterns. A low, round entry hole allows entry to anyone prepared to crouch down. Behind the entrance a wide, courtyard-like interior space opens up, from which several wooden steps lead up to a gallery running almost all the way around. This can be fled to in order to defend the property; underneath, weapons, everyday objects and supplies can be stored and protected from the rain. On the side opposite the entrance, a wooden staircase leads to the house of the village chief, a one-and-a-half-storey building, whose frame is borne by a row of three supporting beams. The family lived elevated on the first floor, above a space for small animals, farming tools and large clay jugs of drinking water. The whole site is surrounded by a palisade. A typical Chin house of the past united living space with other functions: it was simultaneously a defence facility, ritual space, wood store, granary, wagon garage – and it offered space for everyday family life, for threshing, for housework, for celebrations.

Until the British conquered Chin State, in a difficult battle against the reputedly militaristic mountain dwellers that lasted almost a decade, the traditional houses were widespread. New construction methods and provisions led to their disappearance. In the course of the revitalisation of old traditions, not only are former building traditions being revived, but also the handicraft art of ornamentation.

Address 93°35'53.84" E 22°38'11.95" N, Sah-Thah 687, Vel Nang Street, Dillo Quarter, New Bazaar Ward, Hakha | Getting there Around 650 yards east of the Chin Parliament take sharp right behind the State Guest House, or around 250 yards west of the tennis courts turn sharp left into Vel Nang Street, follow the street around 0.6 miles to the fenced-in building on the right side | Tip You can buy beautiful woven Chin wares in shops along Hakha-Matupi and Hakha-Falam Road.

88__Falam Baptist Church
More than religion

The Falam Baptist Church – in Indiana, Michigan, Seattle, Charlotte, Maryland, Oklahoma, Melbourne? No, this is the mother church of them all, the biggest church building in Chin State – in Falam, of course. The building itself is still young, built in 1983, substantially financed through donated money, including from Chin communities abroad. It is the focal point of social life in the town, in which the 10,000 inhabitants live predominantly from local agriculture, trade with the lowlands and nearby India as well as from service-sector work – but in which few income opportunities are on offer, especially for the young.

Falam was the centre of Chin State until the capital was relocated to Hakha in 1974. The locals lament the change to this day, as many jobs have moved too. As a result, the church has become more important as a central place of orientation and cohesion.

There is hardly a family in the cities and towns of Chin State – less so in the villages – of which at least one member hasn't lived, worked or studied abroad. Tensions and unrest, but also the lack of economic opportunity, resulted in migration flows into nearby countries, but especially to 'the West' – to the USA, to Canada, Scandinavia, Germany, Australia. You often hear similar migration stories from the fates of innumerable individuals: the family saved up in order to send the most intelligent, capable son or the cleverest, most hard-working daughter for an education or to study abroad, in the hope that he or she would receive a better-paid position there afterwards, to be able then to send money home. This money secures the education of younger siblings, and the parental household can get by in daily life. This knits the community together, beyond all borders. Since the recent expansion of modern telecommunication links, connections are once again more active.

Address 93°40'40.06" E 22°54'45.84" N, Falam | **Getting there** In the centre of Falam on a spur above Falam Road | **Hours** All day | **Tip** There is an impressive cemetery on a spur beneath Falam Hakha Road, around 2 miles away from the central junction in Falam.

89 Mini Gardens

Greens for the soup

There is not much space in Falam. Streets, houses – everything has to arrange itself in the most cramped of spaces. The slopes are steep and steeper, depending on where you happen to be. On the only 'plateau', a small plain that seems to have slipped down into its position, most of the administration buildings and some residential houses bunch up next to the large building of the Falam Baptist Church; even the market has to make do with a peripheral location a little way below. Many wooden houses stand half on the central road – which was astonishingly widened and 'scratched' into the mountain recently, half over the slope, propped up by six-, sometimes even 26-foot-long, thin wooden posts. You hardly dare imagine how it would be if the stilts and the ground below were swept away by strong monsoon rainfall, which apparently happens sometimes.

As a result, space for everyday life is also rare: space for the bench in front of the house, right by the road, for evening discussions with family and friends; rooms for the residents to spend their time and for setting up the loom; space for the domestic animals and the pigs. Cars hardly played a role here until the recent past – today's road space previously offered sufficient space for crafts, chopping wood, drying clothes, for the children to play. And on every little sliver of land, on almost every corner, space is made for mini gardens. They are dug into the slope, laid out as miniature beds right by the house, cared for, watered. Sometimes a couple of flower pots are enough to make a mini garden.

It is more practical this way: salad, vegetables, herbs, the greens for the soup literally grow in the pot. This place deserves a prize for the fantastic collective effort to make the urban space green, everywhere, on the smallest of plots. Of course, it's very different to back home. The custom is still alive! But for how long? May the principle of keeping the city environs green survive the changing times of auto-mobility, and remain highly valued!

Address 93°40'37.52" E 22°54'44.67" N, Falam | Getting there On houses all over Falam, including on Lower Bogyoke Street below Falam Road in the city centre | Tip Backstrap weavers (*jack khout*) work in shops and private houses along Lower Bogyoke Street.

90 Boarding School

Long journeys, expensive knowledge

From outside it may make you think more of a barn, but it is so lively inside that you're sure to be curious: hundreds of children repeat the alphabet, copying the teacher in unison, loud and clear, engaged and fully concentrated. In the morning you will see pupils in tracksuits all over the town, and once you know they live in simple dormitories, you can recognise the cramped accommodations in which they live. They come from the surrounding villages, some walking several days or riding with their parents on motorbike, over hill and dale, in order to be able to get to school here for a few or – depending on what is financially possible – many months. The boarding schools are especially popular before the conclusion of the 10th year – before the children take the highly prized 'matric exam', the entrance exam for the universities and colleges. The youths take this exam when they are 16 years old. The rest of their further education, ultimately the rest of their lives, depends on the score they achieve: whether they can even go to a university or a college and which subject they are allowed to study. Unlike in Europe, subject preferences hardly play a role; the bachelor's degree as such is what counts. The higher their score, the more prestigious the subject. Repeating years or changing courses is not possible.

The parents are, as a rule, not able to financially shoulder a stay in boarding school on their own, certainly not for their many children. For the best there are scholarships. But often all the relatives or even the whole village will pool their savings in order to enable the most gifted and most hard-working pupils a stay in Falam. It is often the money transferred from relatives abroad that substantially finances the education of younger siblings or cousins. Before long, these students will bear the cost of educating the next generation in their turn. This is an implicit intergenerational contract outside of any state regulation.

Address 93°40'45.48" E 22°54'40.89" N, Falam | Getting there Around 200 yards downhill of the Falam Baptist Church, opposite the Town Hall | Tip Visit the morning market on the central marketplace and eat breakfast afterwards in the Shan Noodle Restaurant right by the town hall.

91___Heart Lake
Cross-border desires

The surface of the water on the heart-shaped Rih Lake, right on the border with India, not only mirrors the raw beauty of the Chin Hills, which are still largely inaccessible. The lake is also a sacred place of the traditional animistic faith of the Chin people, among whom Christianity has spread over the past 100 years. The souls of the dead wandered through the lake on the way to a peaceful stay in the village of the dead (*mitthi khua*, for the normal) or in paradise (*pialral*, for the chosen ones). This notion was widespread.

Due to the parallels with Christianity – especially the belief in a higher power (*mal rhai* and *muihla*) and a life after death – the supposed contradiction between traditional ways of life and Christian concepts is in fact more of an integrative factor for the definition of identity of a people who are divided into six main and numerous sub-clans and are now spread over three territories. According to myth, the Chin were made of the interior of the Earth, *chinlung*. They then are said to have immigrated into the Chindwin valley (northwest Myanmar), relocated to Kamphat at the foot of the Chin Hills due to a flooding catastrophe and were driven by Shan princes into the western mountains all the way to Manipur and Chittagong around the year 1500. The Chin thus developed numerous individual 'social groups' (Tual communities) with their own dialects and gradually different traditions. The loss of their centuries-old independence through the British annexation in 1886, the dissection of their traditional homeland (Chinland), persecution until 2011, and until, recently the lack of stimulus for development led to a revived desire for collective ethnic identity today. Traditional belief and Christianity combine and support community. Cross-border trade is developing, and the Rih Lake is increasingly becoming a tourist destination for Chin from both sides of the border.

Address 93°23'6.72" E 23°20'26.37" N, Rihkhawdar | **Getting there** From Tedim cross Rihkhawdar Block 2 on Tyao River and climb up to Rhikhawdar Block 1 to the lake; from Falam turn left at the entrance of Block 1 | **Tip** A walk through the small, densely built-up second centre of Rihkhawdar on the Tyao border river is worthwhile, but unfortunately it is not possible to cross the border.

92 Laipien Sect
A place of permanent sound

Drumming sounds, celestial sounds, the same melody, by day and by night, always, constant. You can't escape it. And then there is the metal box, large as a house, a mixture of silver, over-sized lunar lander and a UFO from a 1970s' science-fiction film. You look across at it from an octagonal tower with outside steps – an over-sized radio alarm clock, tuned to future sounds. Not far off, memorials with a blue globe, steles with the portrait of a man and the characters of a strange alphabet.

You'll need express consent from the warden to pass through the gates and drive beyond his house. Then you'll go almost half a mile through a regularly built-up settlement with large stone houses, in part colourful and adorned with friezes. You can be excused if you don't immediately grasp that you have entered into the centre of a sect, which by all accounts is said to have an estimated 5,000 disciples following it. It was established on 1 January, 1917 by the prophet Pau Cin Hau, a Chin with a sense of mission, who wanted to pass on the teachings of the all-knowing creator Pasian to his faithful. His Laipien sect pursues deliverance from the evil demon Dawi, in that they renounce the killing of animals and only eat plant products. The teaching combines righteous living with spiritual rituals of the sacred Siangsawn spirits. Their own literature and music is part of this.

The sect was registered by Viscount Chelmsford and is officially recognised in Myanmar to this day. It is rumoured that they even have close friends in external communities who have supported them financially. Devotees construct large buildings for their assemblies, called 'churches', with a kind of altar, without a cross. The sect is represented by small, self-isolated groups, which can be recognised by the sign of the flame in the gable of their churches, in some cities in Chin State.

Address 93°40'14.9" E 23°23'41.81" N, Tiddim | **Getting there** Tiddim can be reached from Kalay (Sagaing Region) on what is now a very well-developed road in around 3.5 hours (50 miles). The Laipien village (Siangsawn Veng) is east of the northern end of the built-up area of Tiddim, accessed via Teeklui Road (around 1 mile from Tiddim Road). | **Hours** Access to the village after registering at the gate | **Tip** You can buy the excellent Chin coffee in the shops on the road in the village. You can only get Tiddim coffee in Tiddim.

93__ Salt Springs
Bubbling out of the Earth

First of all you scoot over hill and down dale on a moped, stride under trees through fields and meadows, and slip through gravel and sand – and then you find the salt for the soup. This is what you may experience in Cikha, if you the leave the 'main road' of the village following the suggestion that there are interesting things to be seen on the ground behind the hill. But before all of that, you first have to have taken a four-day journey: 26 hours in a coach from Yangon, through the plains and over several mountain ranges to Kalay, followed by two day trips through the massif from Chin State to Manipur River. There the journey ends, for the time being. Fortunately, a bridge is currently being built here. Before, you had to cross the river, which has a similar width to the Elbe after light rainfall, but more like that of the Rhein after a storm. Because of the high speed of the current as well as the varying water levels, there are no ferries.

After days of what seem like endless, winding roads, lanes, paths, tracks and unimaginably beautiful landscapes and villages, cool temperatures and cold, always up and down – that's mountains for you! – suddenly a wide, delightfully green valley opens up, with pretty houses lined up along a central road, fresh rice paddies, sunflowers, woods. The temperature rises with every foot of the descent from the mountains. Here you have to be self-sufficient in everything. Including salt.

Blubbering bulges bubble out of the ground, mud makes marching maddening, crystals cause crusts. The salt of the Earth – here it is. Even if it later turns out, in the labs of the University of Cologne, to 'only' be normal salt (sodium chloride) without any special ingredients, it was worth the discovery anyway. And a little later, a short trip to the Indian border can follow: a simple stream, idyllic in the woods. In the mountains beyond is the border post.

Address 93°31'36.09" E 23°53'34.02" N, Cikha | Getting there 80 miles north of Tiddim, around 6 miles from the Myanmar-India border. The salt springs are around 1 mile west of the sports fields, best reached by motorbike via an unsurfaced road. | Tip Drink something cold at the last kiosk before the border in Cikha, not far from the school on the west side of the road. Why not enjoy a bag of homemade potato crisps too?

94__ Border Trade
Mountain-to-mountain business

Monkey fruit is everywhere. Demand in India is high, so after the harvest in April, hundreds of merchants cross the border every day from Myanmar to Manipur, transporting the long green pods from east to west. And not only that. In the market halls right on the border crossing you can buy pretty much everything you already know from the restaurant scene and the shopping paradises of Myanmar's big neighbour: Indian curries and masala, cans of matar paneer and shahi jamun, Indian chai and Himalayan toothpaste, salwar kameez and Kashmir scarfs.

Tamu – complemented on the Indian side by the city of Moreh – has turned into a transhipment point for border trade between India and Myanmar in recent years. From Myanmar it is mainly unprocessed agricultural products, from China cheap plastic goods and from Thailand expensive foods that are brought into India, while finished goods leave India for Myanmar. It would be naive to believe that everything is regulated and registered. It would in any case be a fatuous undertaking to try to control the more than 995-mile-long 'green border'.

Tamu and Moreh are the anchor points of a big idea, namely a continuous good road connection between India and Thailand. India already invested heavily in it some years ago, with support such as the paved motorway, the India Myanmar Friendship Road. Thailand also isn't skimping on the expansion of the motorway from Bangkok via Tak to Mae Sot. In between there's a good 800 miles of road under construction and facing the challenge of finding the best way over and beyond numerous mountain chains – not a question of time, but more of finances and political priorities. And so, for the time being, trade across the border remains a matter on the edge of the states, from one mountain close to the border to another – but not yet much beyond.

Address 94°18'32.87" E 24°14'48.08" N, Tamu | **Getting there** Roughly 3 hours from Kalay on the AH1, the border market (Namphalong) in Moreh is north of the Chaung Gyi River | **Tip** Enjoy a steaming cup of traditional Indian chai in the coffee shops of Namphalung market at the checkpoint.

95___Chindwin Harbour

Five days downstream

There are flights from Mandalay to Khamti only twice a week, already an unmistakable indicator of how far you are going from the centre of the country. And already on the flight over the dense treetops of the extensive forested areas of the Sagaing Region you understand how as yet unexplored the northwest is. Ten minutes before landing, the forest thins out and you fly over cleared areas with countless quarry lakes, fields of rubble, shack settlements – you've arrived in the opencast mining region of Hpakant with the best jade deposits in the world. In Khamti, a small city awaits with a not-so-small market area and a lively riverside road along the levees of the Chindwin River. Its height is astonishing to start with, as the river lies almost 65 feet below. The reports one hears of the enormous volumes of water and floods during the monsoon quickly enhance one's understanding. Deforestation, also as a consequence of mining, leads to increased streamflow.

On the unsecured river harbour – how would one be able to build a fixed pier with such differing water levels after all? – numerous, colourfully and neatly painted boats are strung out, with cabins in the front area, a deeper-lying passenger and load area in the middle, engine room and disposal point at the back, and a flat roof suitable for the transport of goods of all kinds.

Journeys down the Chindwin, via Thamanti, Homalin, Mawlaik and Kalewa to Monywa regularly start from here. If you are ready to start before sunrise, you can cover the distance with an express boat during the dry season in two to three days, depending on the water level and condition of the sandbanks; but it is no mistake to give yourself a bit more time. You can also cover the good 500 miles in a combination of bus, shared taxi and car. That is the adventurous option, of unpredictable duration, during which you quickly realise that roads are not an ideal choice everywhere.

Address 95°41'40.83" E 26°0'9.28" N, Khamti | Getting there In northern Chindwin (Sagaing Region, Khamti Township), only accessible by plane | Tip Enjoy the sunset from the Mya Thein Tan Pagoda in the south of the city at the end of the riverside road.

96__City at the Margin
Deep in the 1,000 mountains

In Myanmar, Nagaland is associated with extremely remote areas, hostile mountain clans and a self-administered zone. To cover the distance of 25 miles as the crow flies between Khamti and Lahe, it takes a good six hours over the five mountain ranges with very steep slopes and often unpaved paths – and that's if the weather is dry. Lahe is actually comparatively the easiest place to get to in Nagaland, which in total stretches over 190 miles along the border with India. The various clans were combative, and not only against each other; they also stand – both west and east of the border – some groups to this day in resistance against the state authorities. With special administrative status they are allowed to make their own laws. Recently, Lahe was officially bestowed the status of city, a privilege that comes with the right to receive a provision of public institutions from the state. Alongside a series of new administration buildings there's also a hospital, a secondary school and a market hall, as well as improved road connections and drainage. With these most recent facilities, Lahe is starting to become a new, small supply centre for the northwest of the country.

The city of Lahe is made out of three parts. In the centre you find small shops and market stalls, in which there are many goods, recently also 'Western' goods, on sale – from tools to clothing to rare goods. A church and pagoda are also located in the centre along with the New Year square for the expressive new year's celebrations. The traditional village is on the edge of the steep slopes; here you will find traditional houses, made of natural materials, often with deep, sagging roofs and always with a surrounding house garden for self-sufficiency. Corrugated iron has seldom found a foothold here, particularly because of the strong downpours and storms during the rainy season but also for financial reasons. Solar panels are increasing in number – they bring light to the night.

Address 95°26'34.27" E 26°19'31.24" N, Lahe | Getting there In the Naga Mountains (3,600 feet above sea level) in the northern Sagaing Region (Lahe Township), only accessible by plane | Tip Trips into the villages of the Naga are recommended, but you'll need an official travel permit, which also determines which villages you can visit.

97 Shwe Myae Zu Pagoda

Shining in the lake

It appears in the distance like a mirage when you cross Indawgyi Lake by motorboat on the way from Lone Ton to the pelicans in the bird sanctuary. As long as no waves from passing or debarking boats disturb the surface of the water, the image and mirror image of the Shwe Myae Zu Pagoda seem identical: a wide white platform swims, so it would seem, in the middle of the lake, and a golden stupa plunges into the blue of the water, just as it pierces the blue of the sky. If you approach from the west, it's only at the last moment that you notice the landing that the boat heads for, from which you can explore the pagoda. And then you also see that the pagoda isn't standing completely in the water, but is connected to the bank around 200 yards away via a secured path. The peace on the artificial island is only disturbed once a year when a several-day celebration at the end of February or the start of March attracts local families, who spend the night on the banks opposite the pagoda and celebrate with loud music.

Indawgyi Lake, at over 46 square miles, is the largest natural lake in Myanmar. The residents of the few villages on the lake are predominantly employed in agriculture and fishing, but often only odd jobs can be found. As a result, many young people with a good school education have a desire to leave the region to look for better employment opportunities. Beyond agriculture and fishing, which so far has mainly served regional self-sufficiency in the west of Kachin State, or gold mining in the bordering mountain ranges, there are currently only modest development possibilities for the approximately 50,000 inhabitants of the region around the lake – a weak economic base that is also threatened by overfishing and signs of environmental destruction. Despite the rural infrastructure, there is, however, a potential for future ecotourism. The first small lodgings rent canoes and bikes for guests to explore the area.

Address 96°18'57.35" E 25°8'56.23" N, Indawgyi Lake | Getting there Around 100 miles west-southwest of Myitkyina (Kachin State, Mohnyin Township), pagoda on west shore of the lake near the village of Nanpade | Tip Take a close-to-nature walk through the settlement of Lone Ton.

98__Lakeside Nature Reserve
Among pelicans and storks

Beautiful birds sail overhead in large flocks. You can hear their squawking, snorting, whooshing and whistling if you are out in a rowboat or have turned off your speedboat motor. In 1999, a 300-square-mile area at the north end of Indawgyi Lake was declared a bird sanctuary. Ninety-five different species of aquatic birds live here, including many migratory birds; ten species are on the red list. Protected species include the green peafowl, the Baer's pochard, the grey pelican, the Malayan stork, the purple swamphen, the lesser adjutant and the white-rumped vulture.

The lake and its immediate surroundings belong, like other areas of Myanmar, to the most species-rich regions in the world, the 25 global hotspots of biodiversity. The north of Kachin, the forests of Kayin State and vast parts of Tanintharyi exhibit the highest biodiversity. Some regions are still hardly researched. The bandwidth of Myanmar's ecosystem stretches from Alpine pastures, dry and rain forests through flooding areas and coastal zones to river deltas, coral reefs and island archipelagos. The species list contains more than 300 mammals, 370 reptiles and 1,089 birds, including many threatened by extinction. Among these are wild elephants (protected since 1879), tigers, leopards, bears, some primates and numerous birds. Other species have already been eradicated, for example the giant panda and several species of rhinoceros.

Myanmar contains seven national parks, three nature reserves and 29 conservation areas, as well as protection zones and elephant camps. There are zoos in Yangon, Mandalay and Nay Pyi Taw. Most of the conservation areas are under pressure from agricultural exploitation, mining and infrastructure development. The problems of law enforcement, insufficient management plans, a shortage of personnel and deficient finances all impede environmental protection, which really deserves that name.

Address 96°22'7.48" E 25°14'2.13" N, Indawgyi Lake | Getting there Northern area of Indawgyi Lake, around 100 miles west of Myitkyina | Tip Take a half-hour trip to Nyaungbin, where there's a large impressive primary school.

99_Jade Mining
Neighbourhood mines and major corporations

The drive to Hpakant first leads through mountainous, picturesque, still barely populated terrain. But soon the picture changes: deforested slopes line ploughed-up landscapes, brown rivers wind through settlements that have clearly been established in a hurry, built in a Wild West manner. It is the new Eldorado for treasure seekers and fortune hunters in Myanmar and an illuminating example of a young mining city.

Mineral maps list, alongside the supposedly finest and largest jade deposits in the world, numerous others, among them very rare minerals such as eckermannite, glaucophane, kosmochlor, richterite, trinepheline and wüstite. The gems and minerals are predominantly extracted in opencast mines. Countless bulldozers, diggers, drilling machines and trucks – many of which have been imported – rummage around in the slopes. The demand for wood for mining and domestic use is high; correspondingly the surrounding forests are extensively cleared. During the monsoon, the living and working conditions are even more extreme. Around 800 mining companies operate under licence in Hpakant, but there are 10 large companies that dominate, which are almost exclusively in Chinese ownership or are joint ventures. Neighbourhoods group around the small mines, where labourers dig for jade with simple tools. Many also search for smaller finds in the loosely piled, and therefore unstable, spoil heaps.

Hpakant has grown outwards enormously in recent years: increasing numbers of migrant workers, mostly young men from nearly all parts of Myanmar, flock into the town on the Uyu River, which was still a very small settlement well into the 1970s. They are looking for a chance to find work here in mining or at least as day labourers. In addition, new mines have been tapped in recent years in the surrounding areas.

Address 96°17′28.5″ E 25°36′41.33″ N, Hpakant | Getting there Around 140 miles west-northwest of Myitkyina on the U Yu Chaung River. An official travel permit is required for the journey from Indawgyi Lake through valleys with deforested slopes. | Tip There is a good view over the old town from Jade City Hotel.

100   Resource Motherlode

Amber by the sheet

Very few tourists make their way into the Hukawng Valley; until now it has been among the least-known destinations in the country. They mostly come to visit the largest tiger reserve in the world, which was declared a conservation area in 2003. The almost 7,000 square miles are also home to numerous other species such as elephants, leopards and bears. The very rare leaf muntjac also lives here. In addition, there are numerous species of monkeys and birds, rare amphibians, reptiles and insects. An estimated 13,500 plant species also add to the enormous diversity.

Tanai is in the centre of the Hukawng Valley, which can be reached on a well-gravelled road from Myitkyina. At first glance it seems to belong to the many small cities of local importance, with a small market and supply centres, well-kept living quarters, a lively little river harbour. But Tanai is much more, namely the centre of one of the most important development fronts in the country. The desires of national and international investors in terms of agriculture and mining are massive. Development of the former Ledo Road between India and China is also being considered.

Even though the local population are often blamed for the decline in the animal population in the conservation area, the problem lies elsewhere: large agricultural companies have obtained permission to grow cassava, jatropha and sugarcane for the production of biofuels for China on an area of 80,000 hectares. Gold mines and gold-panners increasingly operate in opencast mines, for example in western Shingbwiyang Valley. Many use cyanide, mercury, arsenic and cadmium for the extraction of gold, all of which damage the waters and soils. The mining of and trade in amber is also flourishing: the geologist Otto Helm first described the roughly 100-million-year-old fossilised resin in 1894 and named it burmite. You can see it in Tanai where it is mined in large sheets.

101 Shatapru Manau
The dance of independence

In times of peace, the Kachin's traditional Manau celebration takes place in Myitkyina and Puta-O in the first week in January. It brings together Kachin, not only from the various parts of Kachin State and Myanmar, but from all around the world. The Kachin Culture and Literature Central Committee normally organises the celebrations. There is also the Manau Festival Organization Committee, officially engaged by the government of Kachin. This now organises the five-day Manau Dance Festival, in which many members of the administration, business people and some religious organisations take part.

Manau means 'festival' in the Kachin (or more precisely Jinghpaw) language, and the Kachin come together in order to celebrate, wearing their best traditional clothes and carrying weapons in the traditional dances around the Manau stakes. In the past, participants would travel up to four days to get there. The ten Manau stakes (six stand vertical, four diagonal) are painted with colourful motifs: ants, flying birds, fighting bulls, surging waves. The two largest stakes stand for father (with the moon) and mother (with the sun). Six stakes represent the main ethnic groups of the Kachin: the Jinghpaw, Lachit, Lauwo, Lisu, Rawang and Ziawa.

Traditionally there are seven reasons for the Manau: celebrating the new year, a good harvest, a victorious battle, or school or university graduation; to inaugurate a new house or a church; for family parties for weddings; or for the send-off of relatives who are moving to another region. The original reason was the veneration of *Lamu Madai Nat*, the god of spirits, in whom some Kachin still believe to this day. Today the celebration is also in part the expression of the will for a strong ethnic identity. The Manau festival is thus the most important event of the year, at which all the ethnic groups of Kachin State come together.

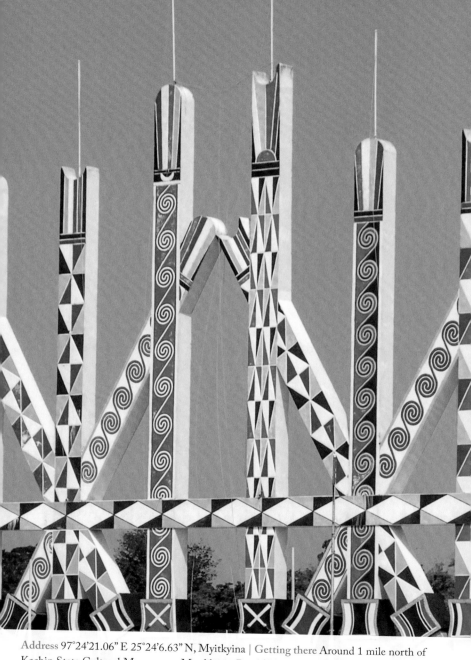

Address 97°24'21.06" E 25°24'6.63" N, Myitkyina | Getting there Around 1 mile north of Kachin State Cultural Museum on Munkhrain Road | Tip A visit to the Kachin Language Society in the northeast corner of the Manau square and the Kachin State Cultural Museum on Munkhrain Road (northwest corner by the stadium) is highly recommended.

102 Ayeyarwady Steps

Everyday life by the river

Steps lead up from the Ayeyarwady to the market. They are not wide, but are still occupied by market sellers offering a large range of local fruit and vegetables, some of which are rare. In this way they represent a connection between the busy city centre and the gently flowing river, which reaches, with the slight gradient here, the considerable width of several hundred yards. The river isn't busy, but hulking freighters or fast passenger boats consistently glide past. They make it clear how much the Ayeyarwady itself is on the periphery of the country for the transport of people and goods. Fruit and vegetables are delivered from the opposite bank, which has not yet been absorbed by urban expansion. Around 350 yards downstream of the steps, restaurants offer the possibility to relax a while with wide terraces. If dining there in the evening, when dusk and darkness spread in a quick changeover, you shouldn't forget to protect yourself against the mosquitoes.

The whole bank of the river is incorporated into everyday life. Around 100 yards upstream, next to another set of steps between the city and the Ayeyarwady, laundry is being washed by a colourfully dressed group of women and children play with pebbles nearby; a little further away the river becomes a bath. A few landings enable boats to deliver directly to the market.

Myitkyina is the capital of Kachin State, the northernmost territory of Myanmar, which reaches all the way to the Hengduan Mountains, which already belong to the Himalayas and have their highest peak in Hkakabo Razi (19,295 feet). The eponymous Kachin (the term lumps together several ethnic groups) were largely Christianised, so that you come across numerous, often very simple churches, not only in Myitkyina, but also in the area's hinterland. Up on the edge of the mountains there are very few settlements, apart from in a sprinkling of basin landscapes with intensive agriculture.

Address 97°24'9.45" E 25°23'8.2" N, Myitkyina | Getting there 550 yards north of the central market on the banks of the Ayeyarwady | Tip Visit the River View restaurant, for typical local food and a river view.

103 Backstrap Weavers
Precious soft woven goods

The woman sits on a mat on the floor, her feet pressed against a block of wood, in her hands the weaving frame of bamboo sticks and twigs: she is using a very old weaving technique – with backstrap and yoke. The women have to sit in fixed positions for long periods. The warp is attached to a rod on a beam on one side, on the other through a yoke near her body; it is tensed using the backstrap of wide leather or a cloth band, which the weaver veritably 'lies into'. The weft is fed through by hand or – depending on the pattern – woven in with the help of a thick porcupine spike. The threads are then rammed down tight with a flat bamboo rod.

The threads of the warp are usually dyed before weaving; cotton is used most of the time. The Kachin favour strong, thick, tightly woven fabrics; in terms of colours, black and bright red are particularly popular. Bright colourful geometric patterns are often woven or embroidered into a black background, which join up to create further, large geometric patterns. Modernised patterns have been added recently, synthetic, bright neon colours are increasingly used and new, partly abstract designs developed.

Longyis and eingyis – the traditional wrap-around skirts and blouses – as well as scarves, drapes, sling bags and small pieces such as purses, containers and dolls are woven. Kachin woven goods are among the best and most expensive clothing in Myanmar, but they are also very long lasting. Backstrap woven longyis occupy the upper price segments. Because the woven webs are naturally relatively narrow, three webs are sewn together horizontally in their production; the patterns of the webs must also be carefully matched. A weaver takes six to eight weeks to produce one such web. Weaving is a woman's world, and in the past was also combined with ritual acts, particularly as the fabrics and patterns were of cultural as well as social importance in village life.

Address 97°24'45.74" E 25°25'20.74" N, Myitkyina | Getting there 15-minute walk to the districts northeast of Myitkyina University | Tip There are numerous churches to see in Myitkyina; some façades are completely decorated with pebbles.

104 Aluminium Recycling

What a can can do

What to do with all the old drinks cans? That the aluminium they are made of is a valuable raw material can be learned in this small, family-run operation, in which used cans and other aluminium waste are made into pans, bowls and other kitchenware. They are sold to the local population.

The production process seems to be actually simple: the used cans and other aluminium scrap are melted down and the desired objects cast with the liquid molten metal. But this largely manual process requires lots of skill. The biggest challenge is the creation of the sand mould for the cast. Let's imagine the production of an aluminium bowl: the sand mould for this is made up of two parts and is created with the help of a model. The lower part of the mould is made by pressing moist sand into a bowl that serves as a model and then covering it with a wooden box. Both are turned upside down and the bowl is carefully removed so that a full mould of sand remains in the box. For the top box, sand is filled around the model and solidified before the model is removed. Now the upper box must be carefully placed on top of the lower box, with core marks aiding guidance. The two parts of the mould are fitted together exactly on two wooden guides, so that the bowl can be cast with the opening at the bottom.

So that the very fine mould sand is easily modelled and the mould holds, it is dampened slightly. Any crumbling away would lead to a weak point or even a hole in the wall of the bowl. Once the mould parts are lying precisely on top of each other, the cast can be made. Every cast is a one-off – the principle of metal casting in a lost mould. At the end, any irregularities on the cast and cooled bowl are eliminated on a vertical turntable, before the edges are cleaned by hand and rounded off with a file. The aluminium shavings this creates are also collected, melted down and used again for the next cast.

Address 97°23'58.77" E 25°22'00.43" N, Wet Gone Ward, Myitkyina | Getting there Around 1 mile from the central market south on Munkhrain Road, take the fifth bigger road to the right after the railway compound, then the first residential road to the left in the middle of the block | Tip Visit the very beautiful, lively night market in the central market between Munkhrain Road and the riverbank road.

105 Shingra Hpang Htingnu

A house defies the dam

Those taken along to visit relatives by Kachin friends will experience what tremendous significance family and social cohesion have for the Kachin. First of all, they always talk about the family – who is currently doing what and how they are getting on. Precise knowledge about each other, how and who is related directly or by marriage to whom, is a simple matter of course. The extended family is more important than the nuclear family. Unlike most other ethnic groups in Myanmar, the Kachin bear family names. People with the same surname are not allowed to marry.

Families are large and live under one roof; alongside husband, wife and children, the household also includes the parents and other older people of the same lineage. So the Kachin traditionally built large rectangular longhouses – like the one you can see in Myitsone. A house stands on short stilts, has a supporting central post and a series of outer posts and access at both ends. Wickerwork walls divide individual rooms from one another. The floor is made out of layers of bamboo with a sunken box for open fireplaces in a sand bed. In every longhouse there are several fireplaces, *daps*, around which people gather. A large open canopy over the entrance area on the ground level protects against sun and rain; here you can work or play outdoors yet stay protected. The house is entered via a ladder. Several rooms, each with its own fireplace, follow on from a veranda – for the shrine, the family of the children, guests – and a central area with the fireplace for cooking and wall racks for tubes of drinking water. The longhouse in Myitsone was supposed to leave this place, as were the surrounding settlements, to make way for a large dam project funded by Chinese investors, but the project was stopped in 2011. The stone columns commemorate the history.

Address 97°30'10.06" E 25°42'48.95" N, Myitsone | Getting there Around 200 yards east of Myitsone Pagoda at the confluence of the N'Mai Hka and Mali Hka rivers. | Tip On the way to the confluence of the two rivers you will see beautiful little rice-field valleys and slash-and-burn agriculture.

106__ Source of the Ayeyarwady

Pebbles, gold-panners, hydropower

In Myitsone, the N'Mai Kha and Mali Kha rivers flow together and from here bear the name Ayeyarwady. This point is considered the source of the river with the greatest length, largest volume and greatest importance in Myanmar, and attracts many visitors as a mystical place. A Kachin house constructed in a traditional building style and a pagoda represent the location's spiritual importance, while a couple of plain restaurants, safe from flooding on a natural terrace around 65 feet above the river, satisfy the traveller's refreshment needs - spirituality and relaxation come together in one place.

The visitor is quickly drawn to the pebble riverbank. Depending on the mineral composition, the pebbles reveal the very varied origins of the material to the knowledgeable; but their variety also delights the amateur. The power of the transporting water becomes clear on the rounding of the pebbles; with a little patience you can find almost perfectly spherical stones. The sand that the river carries out of the mountains contains gold dust. Not surprisingly, some gold-panners have temporarily settled on the sediment of the valley, trying in the simplest possible way to extract tiny grains of gold from the sand. Wealth isn't to be expected, but you never know …

Long boats glide by on both of the headwaters, often loaded with goods that supply the settlements above to the basin of Puta-O or transport workers. A Chinese company had planned the construction of a huge dam with a hydroelectric power plant downstream of the confluence; the electricity produced was mainly to be exported to China. The project would have required the resettlement of 15,000 people, and the risk of earthquakes is not to be underestimated either. In 2011, the then president stopped the project, whose future is now in the balance.

Address 97°30'11.06" E 25°42'43.78" N, Myitsone | Getting there Pebble shore at the Myitsone Pagoda by the confluence of the N'Mai Hka and Mali Hka rivers | Tip More than anywhere else in Myanmar, take your time to watch the steady flow of the water or the rapid passing of boats, right on the shore or in a restaurant above the steep banks.

107   Fort Hertz

Those with the overview

Only very few walls of the earlier building are still standing, and they have been changed by a later conversion into an almost unrecognisable condition, but they still give you a sense of the defensive power that the old fort would have demonstrated. The British couldn't have picked a better location: once the rampant vegetation on the hill was removed, there was a clear view of the vast plain of Puta-O over the Nam Pa Lak River, so the fort must have seemed like a fortification on a bastion with a sloping bank in front – completely in line with traditional defence engineering – to the colonial powers.

The hill on which the former fort stands enables today's visitor to cast a view over the largely unpopulated plain, which is used for agriculture where it is not traversed by the Nam Pa Lak with its highly different water levels depending on the season. Despite it appearing like a small trickle in the dry season, the river grows dramatically when the rains come. In the flood zone one can, with effort, protect small garden areas from the scree that is carried along by the river during the strong monsoonal rains and is spread out over the area. The hill with the former fort thus also protects the residential areas on the other side from flooding.

Puta-O had great strategic importance in the British colonial era. It was founded back then as Fort Hertz, named after the regional officer William Axel Hertz, who mapped the area in 1888. Seen from India, from where the 'Farther Indian' territories of the United Kingdom were governed into the early 20th century, the small fortress was an outpost in the northern region of 'independent clans' bordering Upper Burma. It was east of the Himalayan spur that divides the river systems of Brahmaputra and Ayeyarwady from each other, and controlled the Ledo or Stilwell Road to China. Today, only the modest remains of the walls of the fort that was rebuilt later remind us of its strategic importance in colonial times.

Address 97°24'3.91" E 27°21'13.48" N, Puta-O | Getting there The fort is on a raised plateau above the flood plain rice fields between the districts of Ho Khu in the north and Kawngahtawn in the south, around 3 miles northwest of the airfield. Beware: Puta-O can only be reached by airplane, and a travel permit must be obtained.| | Tip There are numerous exciting old bridges to see in and around Puta-O.

108 Morning Market
Breakfast on a banana leaf

The cool morning mist creeps through you, down to the marrow. It's good that there are such things as warm jackets and hats. The visitors to the market, doing their morning shopping, seem shivery and half asleep. The first stalls open shortly before sunrise: flat, waist-high bamboo frames, partly covered with plastic sheets, on which fresh vegetables – banana trunk, bitter squash, butter beans, frangipani, rosella, Indian mustard, tamarind leaves, taro, water spinach or lemon grass – and fresh local fruit are offered for sale. Most delicious are the fresh sweet grapefruits, oranges, pineapples and quinces. As fertilisers and agrochemicals are unaffordable for most farmers, most of the products, at least the local ones, are genuinely organic. Many mothers, with their children cosily wrapped up against the cold, swing their shopping energetically into their back carriers woven out of rattan or flat strips of bamboo.

Early in the morning, you will soon notice that markets are not only places for buying and selling, but also offer regional culinary specialities, some of which you won't find in a normal restaurant.

Especially busy and clearly popular among customers of all age groups are the stands that sell steamed dim sum – 'heart's delight' – for example, dumplings filled with shrimp paste or yeast dumplings with lotus seed mash. But the traditional Kachin breakfast enjoys even greater demand: steamed vegetables, often okra and aubergine, mixed with sticky rice mash, garnished with lots of coriander and parsley, seasoned with local herbs and chilli sauce – and then fresh tofu or pieces of rice or pumpkin pudding baked in a little oil. The breakfast is traditionally served on a banana leaf.

Lots of vegetables and rice, but little oil, are generally used in all traditional Kachin dishes. Fish or beef are also used, like in *shan hkak*: minced beef with garlic, basil, ginger, chillies and pepper. A fantastic lunch!

Address 97°24'4.79" E 27°20'31.5" N, Puta-O | Getting there The small market takes place in Kawngahtawn, around 2 miles northwest of the airfield on the road to the old fort, southwest of Taung Tan Kyaung monastery. Beware: Puta-O can only be reached by airplane, and a travel permit must be obtained. | Hours Daily from just before sunrise to late morning | Tip From Puta-O you can take interesting trips to villages with different ethnic groups.

109__One-Way Bridge
Too narrow for two mopeds

The last mile of the journey to the small administrative centre of Machanbaw, around one-hour's drive from Puta-O, can only be done on foot or by motorbike over an imposing steel-and-wood suspension bridge. The 200-yard-long bridge is so narrow and delicate that no car can drive over it, and the space is even too tight for two motorbikes to pass by each other. But the frequency of traffic is rarely so high that this is seen as a particular obstacle. North of Myitkyina there are very few modern bridges crossing over the source rivers of the Ayeyarwady. The area is sparsely populated, but in the vicinity of India and China, every transportation facility is of great importance. Correspondingly the bridges and river crossings are usually very sturdily built so that they can also withstand the increased run-off during monsoon season.

Predominantly local ethnic groups live in Machanbaw, especially Rawang, Kachin and Lisu, but also Khamti Shan as well as Burmese from central Myanmar, who are mostly delegated here as civil servants.

Machanbaw was a settlement outpost and was located, in the time of British exploitation, in the north of Kachin State. It was, from 1913, before Fort Hertz was founded to the north in Puta-O in 1925, the most northerly colonial administrative focal point. The far north was proscribed as a pioneer frontier, but also as a 'place of exile': officers and administrative personnel were sent here for the purpose of punishment or discipline. The remnants of the colonial epoch are still unmissable to this day: numerous former houses of British officers, a British clubhouse and many administration buildings dominate the cityscape, some intact and used by current administrative bodies, others abandoned and in an almost romantic way, left to their own fate. Locals claim that some are haunted by restless spirits.

Address 97°34'58.19" E 27°16'23.33" N, Machanbaw | Getting there Over Mali Hka River, around 12 miles east of Puta-O airfield | Tip Old British administration buildings are preserved around 400 yards northeast of the market (97°35'17" E, 27°17'08" N).

110 Forest Clearing
Monkey business on a jungle path

In the north of Kachin State there remain self-contained forest stands preserved in their extensively primal form, as they have hardly been influenced by mankind thus far. They are among Asia's last large forest areas. The stunted subtropical monsoon forests here are shorter than the evergreen tropical rainforests. In the dry season they dry out, as the trees shed their leaves when faced by a lack of rainfall. The canopy is thin and relatively open, so the forest floor is also drier. As such, more light also reaches the ground, and the undergrowth is denser. The forests are accordingly hard to walk through.

The inhabitants of Avadam use the forest for logging for their own use – as timber for houses and bridges as well as firewood for heating in the cold season and for cooking on their open fireplaces. They also receive an annual reward as compensation for not exploiting the forests for the sale of firewood to other parts of the country or for the production of charcoal, as is the case in some other parts of Myanmar. The forest is of course also used for hunting – for example of birds, squirrels and porcupines – and for the gathering of plant resources, also only for their own use. In light of the sparse population, the forests are hardly affected. The forests are therefore not completely impenetrable, but criss-crossed by a loose network of paths, which the locals know very well.

On a hike through the mountains, which is only possible in the cold dry season, the openness of the forests stands out immediately. There is foliage all over and you can see right into the depths of the forest and up through the canopy. A myriad of birdcalls can be made out, varying at different times of day, you will also hear the excited screeching of troops of monkeys. You can hear them everywhere in the forests and sometimes see them jumping among the branches. They are an unmistakable sign of the fact that the forests here are still intact.

Address 97°8'0.33" E 27°31'38.04" N | **Getting there** The village of Avadam can only be reached on foot, and is around 22 miles northwest of Puta-O on Nam Lang River, 3,120 feet above sea level. The monkey jungle is around 1.5 miles upstream of Avadam. | **Tip** Find yourself a local guide who is familiar with the villages and forests.

111_ The Last Village
Not the end of the world

From Puta-O there is a hiking route that leads to Ziyadam, the 'last village'. It takes four days to complete the roundtrip route. The name of the village is to be understood literally to start with: along a roadway developed during the British era, modest remains of whose route can still be made out, it is the last permanently settled place before Indian territory begins behind the next mountain range. It could also be the last village in another sense: population pressure among the smaller ethnic minorities of the north, the Rawang and Lisu, forced the villagers to take to the peripheral mountainous country, whose accessibility is very difficult, in the early 20th century. Now migration is happening once again, this time out of the mountain settlements.

Ziyadam spreads out on a terrace over the Ziya River. The 'village road' is followed by houses built in the regionally widespread manner of construction: resting on stilts, accessed by steps, the house usually only has three rooms, of which the largest can be heated by an open fireplace in the middle. Despite the altitude (3,495 feet), in which the temperature can fall below freezing during the cold season, the walls are only made of thin wickerwork. The morning fire in the house is lit inside a square sand bed; as the houses have no chimneys or flues, you sit in acrid smoke. Water is taken from a small rivulet or has to be fetched from the river. The large yard area is the daily common room for residents and domestic animals.

The economic possibilities for the population are limited. Some wood can be extracted from the forests and processed; in the valleys a bit of arable farming on a subsistence basis is possible. It is also the 'last village' for tourism, as the accommodation capacity of the houses is minimal. If you leave the village and head towards the mountains you will quickly find yourself surrounded by what appears to be untouched nature.

Address 97°5'58.46" E 27°34'17.33" N, Ziyadam | **Getting there** Around 6 miles northeast of Avadam, 28 miles northeast of Puta-O, at 3,280 feet altitude and only accessible by foot | **Tip** A hike north through tall meadows, leads to the confluence of two rivers with strong currents, in which large stones give a sense of the power of the rainy-season flow.

Bibliography

The following bibliographic references pursue the double purpose of stating the background material for the texts in this book as well as suggesting further reading. We have excluded pure travel literature (architecture and travel guides) and large-format photographic books from the list.

Adas, M. (1974): The Burma Delta: Economic Development and Social Change on an Asian Rice Frontier, 1852–1941. Madison.

Aung-Thwin, M., M. Aung-Thwin (2012): A History of Myanmar since Ancient Times. Traditions and Transformations. London.

Bender, F. (1983): Geology of Burma. Beiträge zur regionalen Geologie der Erde 16. Stuttgart.

Bruns, A. R. H. (2006): Burmese Puppetry. Bangkok.

Cheesman, N., Skidmore, M., T. Wilson (Eds.) (2012): Myanmar's Transition. Openings, Obstacles and Opportunities. Singapore.

Diran, R. K. (1997): The Vanishing Tribes of Burma. New York.

Egreteau, R., F. Robinne (Eds.) (2016): Metamorphosis. Studies in Societal and Political Change in Myanmar. Singapore.

Fraser, D. W., B. G. Fraser (2005): Mantles of Merit. Chin Textiles from Myanmar, India and Bangladesh. Bangkok.

Fraser-Lu, S. (1994): Burmese Crafts. Past and Present. Kuala Lumpur.

Furnivall, J. S. (1957): An Introduction to the Political Economy of Burma. Rangoon.

Golloch, A. (2014): Handwerkskunst in Myanmar (Burma). Mit traditioneller Technik zu Meisterwerken. Aachen.

Gutman, P. (2001): Burma's Lost Kingdoms. Splendours of Arakan. Bangkok.

Hauff, M. von (2007): Economic and Social Development in Burma / Myanmar. The Relevance of Reforms. Marburg.

Hla Tun Aung (2003): Myanmar. The Study of Processes and Patterns. Yangon: National Centre for Human Resource Development, Publishing Committee, Ministry of Education Yangon.

Khin Maung Nyunt (2016): The Historic Bells of Yangon. Yangon.

Köster, U., Phuong Le Trong, Ch. Grein (Hg.) (2014): Handbuch Myanmar: Gesellschaft, Politik, Wirtschaft, Kultur, Entwicklung. Berlin.

Kraas, F. (2009): Tsunami 2004 und Zyklon "Nargis" 2008. Katastrophenbewältigung in den Küstenregionen von Myanmar. Geographische Rundschau 61 (12): 50–58.

Kraas, F. (2016): Ökonomische Transformationen im Delta des Ayeyarwady / Myanmar. Geographische Rundschau 68 (7/8): 24–29.

Kraas, F. (2016): Rubine und Saphire: Zur Entwicklung der Bergbaustadt Mogok / Myanmar. In: Die Welt verstehen – eine geographische Herausforderung. Eine Festschrift der Geographie Innsbruck für Axel Borsdorf. Innsbrucker Geographische Studien 40: 95–118.

Kraas, F., Hlaing Maw Oo, R. Spohner (2014): Yangon Urban Heritage: 189 Listed Heritage Buildings. An annotated thematic map. Cologne. 2nd edition.

Kraas, F., Mi Mi Kyi, Win Maung (Eds.) (2016): Sustainability in Myanmar. Southeast Asian Modernities 15. Wien.

Kraas, F., R. Spohner, Aye Aye Myint et al. (2017): Socio-Economic Atlas of Myanmar. Stuttgart.

KTAM Report (Knappen Tippets Abbett McCarthy Engineers) (1953): Economic and Engineering Development of Burma. Vol. 1: Introduction, Economics and Administration, Agriculture and Irrigation, Transportation. Vol. 2: Telecommunications, Power, Industry. Aylesbury / London.

Kyaw Nyunt Lwin, Khin Ma Ma Thwin (2005): Birds of Myanmar. Bangkok.

Leider, J. P. (2004): Le Royaume d'Arakan, Birmanie. Son histoire politique entre le début du XVe et la fin du XVIIe siècle. Paris.

Ma Thanegi (2008): Myanmar Marionettes. Yangon.

Miksic, J. N., G. Y. Goh (2017): Ancient Southeast Asia. New York.

Mitchell, A. (2018): Geological Belts, Plate Boundaries and Mineral Deposits in Myanmar. Amsterdam.

MLF (Ministry of Livestock and Fishery) (2014): Marine Conservation in Myanmar. Current knowledge and research recommendations. Yangon.

Moilanen, J., Ozhegov, S. S. (1999): Mirrored in Wood. Burma's Art and Architecture. Bangkok.

MoIP (Ministry of Immigration and Population) (2015): The 2014 Myanmar Population and Housing Census. Highlights of the Main Results. Census Report Volume 2-A. Nay Pyi Taw.

Moore, E. (2007): Early Landscapes of Myanmar. Bangkok.

MoPF (Ministry of Planning and Finance) (2016): Myanmar Statistical Yearbook 2016. Nay Pyi Taw.

Nijman, V., Indenbaum, R. A. (2017): Golden Rock Revisited: Wildlife for sale at Kyaiktiyo, Myanmar. TRAFFIC Bulletin 29 (2): 80–84.

Nijman, V., Shepherd, C. R. (2017): Ethnozoological assessment of animals used by Mon traditional medicine vendors at Kyaiktiyo, Myanmar. Journal of Ethnopharmacology 202: 101–106.

Nishizawa, N. (1991): Economic Development of Burma in Colonial Times. IPSHU Research Report Series No. 15. Hiroshima.

O'Connor, S. (1907): Mandalay and other Cities of the Past in Burma. Reprint 1996. Bangkok.

Odaka, K. (Ed.) (2016): The Myanmar Economy. Its Past, Present and Prospects. Tokyo.

Pearn, B. R. (1939): A History of Rangoon. Rangoon.

Percival, B. (2016): Walking the Streets of Yangon. Yangon.

Rabinowitz, A. (2001): Beyond the Last Village. A Journey of Discovery in Asia's Forbidden Wilderness. Washington.

Robin, K. (Ed.) (2009): Chin. History, Culture and Identity. New Delhi.

Sai Aung Tun (2009): History of the Shan State. From Its Origins to 1962. Bangkok.

Sakhong, L. H. (2003): In search of Chin identity. A study in Religion, Politics and Ethnic Identity in Burma. Copenhagen.

Saul, J. (2005): The Naga of Burma. Their Festivals, Customs, and Way of Life. Bangkok.

Schlüssel, R. (2002): Mogok. Eine Reise durch Burma zu den schönsten Rubinen und Saphiren der Welt. München.

Singer, N. F. (1995): Old Rangoon. City of the Shwedagon. Gartmore.

Skidmore, M. (Ed.): (2005): Burma at the Turn of the 21st Century. Honolulu.

South, A. (2008): Ethnic Politics in Burma. States of conflict. London.

Stadtner, D. M. (2011): Sacred Sites of Burma. Myth and Folklore in an Evolving Spiritual Realm. Bangkok.

Su Su, Win Kyaing (2016): 2.000 Years of Urban Continuity in Sri Ksetra-Pyay. In: Kraas, F., Mi Mi Kyi, Win Maung (Eds.) (2016): Sustainability in Myanmar. Southeast Asian Modernities 15. Wien: 307–318.

Taylor, R. H. (2009): The State in Myanmar. London.

Thant Myint-U (2011): Where China Meets India. Burma and the New Crossroads of Asia. London.

Zin Mar Than (2017): Socio-Economic Development of Indawgyi Lake, Myanmar. Stuttgart.

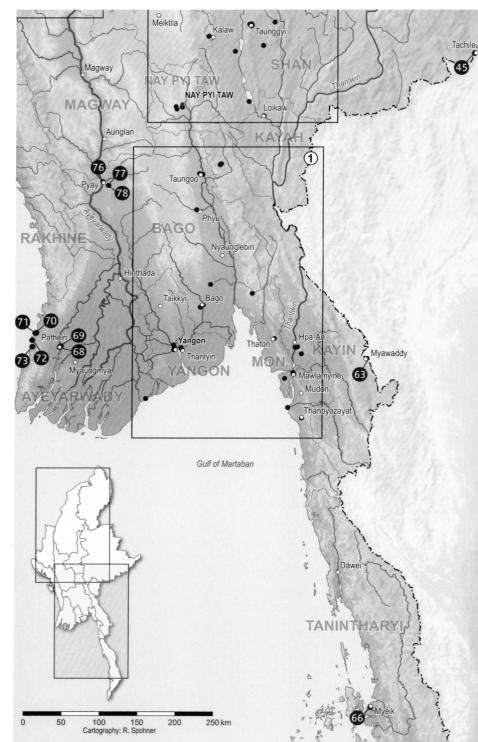

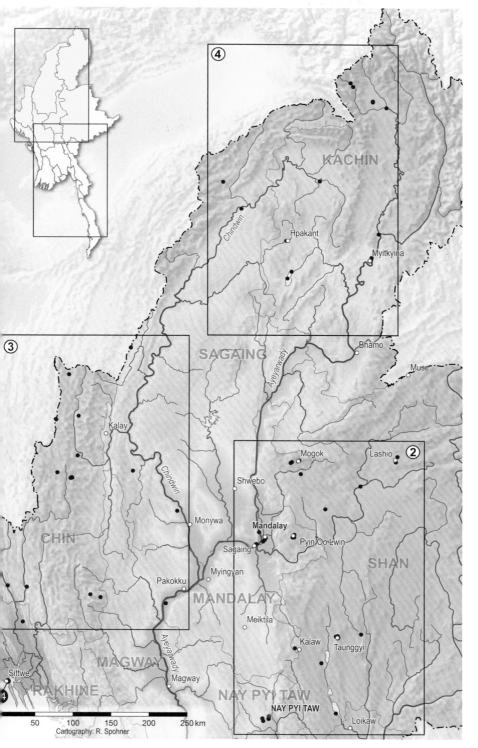

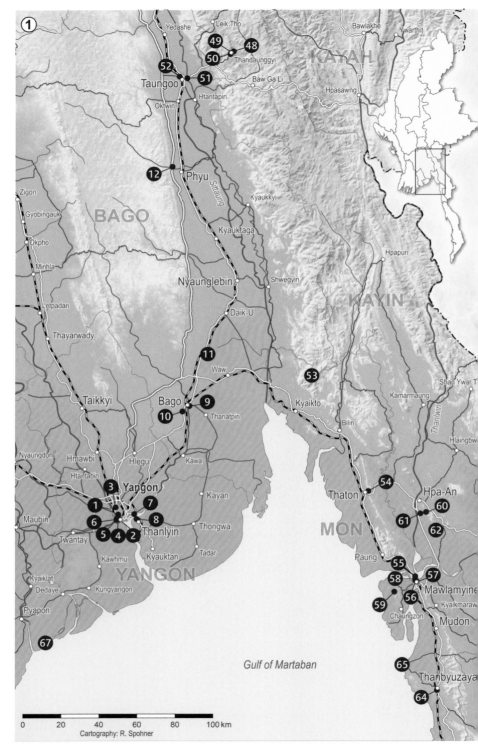

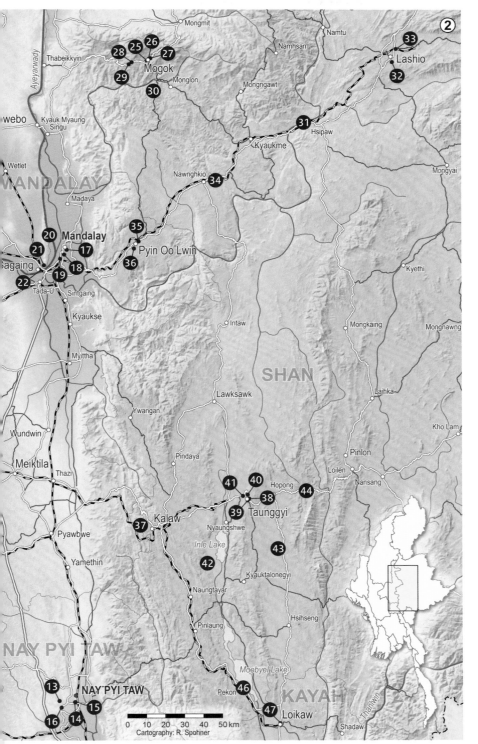

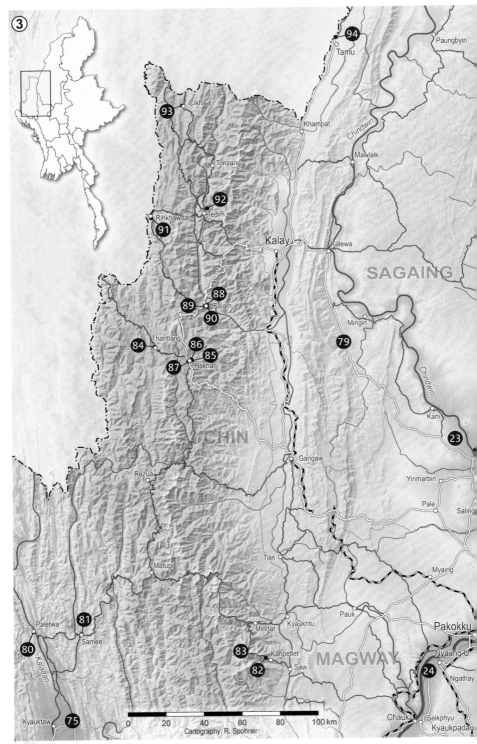

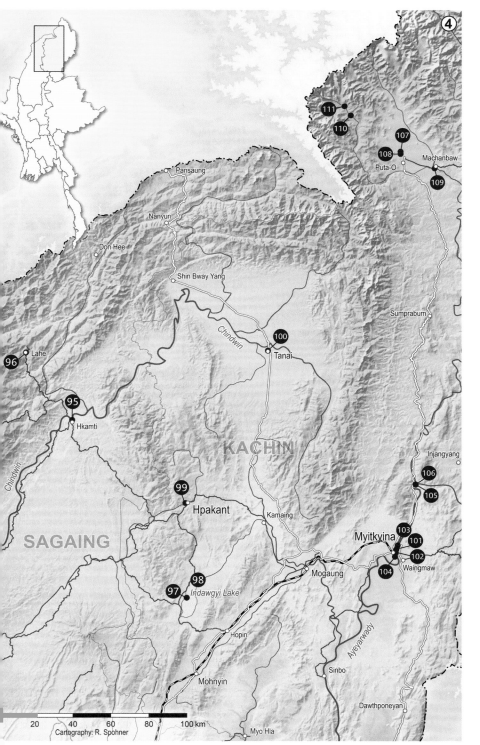

Frauke Kraas studied geography, biology, ethnology and philosophy, finished her doctorate in Münster in 1991, qualified with a habilitation in Bonn in 1996 and has been a professor of urban and social geography at the University of Cologne since 2000. She has worked in Myanmar since 1996, at one point living there for two years, and has travelled throughout the whole country within the framework of several research projects.

Regine Spohner studied cartography and geography in Karlsruhe, Cologne and Bonn, finished her doctorate in Bonn in 2004 and has been a research assistant at the Institute of Geography in Cologne since 2004. She works on research projects on Myanmar and has visited the country in this capacity numerous times.

Jörg Stadelbauer studied geography, history and Latin, finished his doctorate in 1972 and qualified for his habilitation in 1979. From 1987 to 1991 he held a professorship in Mainz, and from 1991 to 2009 he was professor of cultural geography and regional studies at the University of Freiburg. The focuses of his work are cultural geography, Russia, the Caucasus and Central Asia. He has travelled around Myanmar several times since 1996.